ALONG THE WAY

SUBMITTED BY
CARL A. RUNK

Copyright © 2013 Carl A. Runk
All rights reserved.
ISBN: 1483987000
ISBN 13: 9781483987002

Along the Way
Foreword

When you hear the name as Carl Runk, the first image that comes to mind is that of the highly successful championship-winning lacrosse coach at the University of Arizona, Towson University, and Hereford High School, in Baltimore, Maryland. That is just one of the many things that this most fascinating character has mastered. Few folks know that Carl is also proficient at sign language, where he started the program and taught at Towson University. Even less are aware that he is a much sought after public speaker. Carl served as the Master of Ceremonies at the United States Lacrosse Coaches Association Convention for 28 years. And next to no one would believe that he can sing and write music!

At first glance, this very large man projects a rather intimidating presence. However, just a few moments into a conversation will reveal the true personality of this gentle person. For all of his remarkable talents, clearly the most entertaining is his ability to tell a story. When you read this collection of tales, I know you will have a smile on your face and gain an even greater appreciation of this unique individual.

Dick Edell
Former lacrosse coach,
Maryland University

Dedication

This book is dedicated to an individual who, besides his many contributions to the game of lacrosse, has taught us the meaning of love and life-time friendship. Dick Edell is a unique individual who is loved and respected by all those who have been blessed to know him. I consider myself very fortunate to call him my friend.

Acknowledgements

"Along the Way", has been a memorable pleasure to put into words. It is a collection of humorous stories that I, and other coaches, have experienced over the years. It was through the encouragement, unselfishly offered, from my friend, Dick Edell, that the decision to proceed in this direction was made. These beautiful and refreshing experiences have been an opportunity to re-visit and recall entertaining times in my life with my many friends in the coaching profession, along with many other personal friends. As an active participant, I have always taken my responsibilities quite seriously. As a coach, I worked diligently to be successful in improving my teaching skills in the game of lacrosse and football, as well as my association with young people. I was fortunate to receive impeccable advice from Dick Watts, a fellow coaching associate, in my early years, which became a vital part of my philosophy. It was simply to "work extremely hard at your craft, do the best that you can with the young men that you have at that time, and above all, don't take yourself seriously!" Though he probably wasn't aware of it, his guidance was extremely helpful to me throughout my career and I thank him for it.

I would like to thank, first of all, the coaches who contributed to this manuscript. Secondly, I would be remorse if I didn't recognize my many friends and relatives who were also so helpful in its completion. The highly enthusiastic Karen Bathras, an outstanding female lacrosse official, in the men's game, should be given credit for her participation in the completion of the cover, along with my son, Keith Runk. They both were very patient with me at a crucial time and I am truly appreciative.

If, for some reason, you the reader, are involved in one of the episodes and feel you have been misquoted or misrepresented, please take a quarter and call someone who cares! As for me, I won't answer my phone. This is how I remember the stories and I'm sticking to it!

Carl Runk

Table of Contents

1. Mel Fernwacker..........................ix
2. The Nonpareil Truffles....................1
3. Fun Loving Blue Jay......................3
4. The Bank Rest Stop......................5
5. Kids will do the Darndest Things..........9
6. A Teaching Technique...................11
7. Just doing His Job......................13
8. Whose Got # 24.........................15
9. Another Time............................17
10. Like You Fell out of a Plane..............19
11. Learning from the Experienced..........21
12. The Starting Pistol......................23
13. The Styrofoam Bricks....................25
14. Coaching Your Own.....................27
15. My Old Friend Danny...................29
16. Old Buck Taylor.........................33
17. A Gift from Willie Cooper................37
18. Old Buck...............................39
19. Remembering the "Lords" Prayer........41
20. Take off Today..........................43
21. How to Strengthen Your Wrist...........47
22. Where is Coach Hart....................49
23. Big Bad John...........................51
24. St. Patricks' Day Game..................55
25. He's going to be a Good One............57
26. The Speech Impediment.................59
27. The "Van Heusen" Shirt.................61
28. The Colonel and Buck...................63

29.	Chic	67
30.	The Beer Salesman	69
31.	The Double Talker	71
32.	Bill Metzger	73
33.	Mox	75
34.	Frankie Hagan	77
35.	"Ta-Coopa-Coopa"	79
36.	The Hamburger Squad	83
37.	Want to Share the Bill	85
38.	The Navy/Army Game	87
39.	Tire Size 30-45=15's	89
40.	Bob Holcombs' call to Leo	91
41.	The Last Ten Out	93
42.	Mr. John Black	95
43.	The Soothsayer	99
44.	Coach Ron	101
45.	Pearl Harbor	103
46.	"Watch" What You Do	105
47.	The Ultimate Sacrifice	107
48.	Towson School Song	109
49.	The Coke Machine	111
50.	Joe Sugai	113
51.	My favorite Referee Story	115
52.	Lee Pinney's Farm	117
53.	The Scholarship Candidate	119
54.	Old Blood and Guts	121
55.	Defenseman Found Not Guilty	123
56.	Game Plan ... "Stop the Gaits!"	125
57.	The Official with No Sense of Humor	127
58.	Bad Call at Denison	129
59.	The 25 lb. Cone	133
60.	Coca Cola Six Pack	135
61.	The Secret Hiding Place (part 1)	137
62.	Uncle Leo's Abdominal Problems	139
63.	The Secret Hiding Place (part 2)	141
64.	That's not a Knee Pad	143
65.	Knute Rockne?	145

Table Of Contents

66.	The Mile and a Half Run	147
67.	Full Field Ride	149
68.	Divine Intervention?	151
69.	Fancy Panties	153
70.	Another Time	155
71.	The Little Ball Collector	157
72.	Good Athletes are Hard to Come By	159
73.	Coach is Trying to Tell Us Something - Don't Lose!	161
74.	Longest Shot	163
75.	What are the Chances!!!	165
76.	What's a "Broad?"	167
77.	Back up the Goals	169
78.	The Need for a New Bus Driver	171
79.	Where's The Coach of the Year	173
80.	Where is Your Allegiance	175
81.	Two Speakers ... One Banquet	177
82.	If We're Going, We're Going Down Swinging!	179
83.	Refreshments at the Ball Game	183
84.	Hey # 62 ... You Suck!	185
85.	Don't Go Out With Lacrosse Players	187
86.	Billy, the Navy Mascot	189
87.	Wrong Goal, Son!	191
88.	Penalty in the Snow	193
89.	Can You Guess What I'm Thinking	195
90.	Half Time Boxing Match	197
91.	My Son Deserves a Full Ride	201
92.	Your missing a Great Game	203
93.	Sport Pyschology	205
94.	Road Trip to Remember	207
95.	The Penalty Not Called	209
96.	A Memory of Ed Purcell	211
97.	"I Don't Care - I Don't Care	215
98.	Sheepish Tony	217
99.	Getting "Homered"	219
100.	The First "Highlight Film"	221
101.	Right Game ... Wrong Ball	223
102.	Santa Barbara Streaker	225

103.	Pantless Goalkeeper	227
104.	What was I thinking	229
105.	A "McCallism"	231
106.	Dedicated Film Watching	233
107.	What Coaches won't do to win a Game!!	235
108.	House for Sale	237
109.	Recruit Seymour Pablogotz	239
110.	Bob Gucwa … the Referee	241
111.	Officiating at Navy	243
112.	"No Check-Offs"	245
113.	The Toothless Situation	247
114.	Through a Players Eyes	249
115.	Tucson, the Health Capital of the World	251
116.	The Bee Sting	253
117.	Should you tell the truth?	255
118.	Bathroom Leakage	257
119.	Lou Who??	259
120.	Another Story	261
121.	J. D. Davis	265
122.	A Slug of Mouthwash	269
123.	An Anxious Young Coach	271
124.	3 in 1 Oil	273
125.	The Hoagie Eater	275
126.	The Coconut Pie	277
127.	Special Plays Work	279
128.	Playing with the Official	281
129.	The Official Look-Alikes	283
130.	Your Responsible for your own Set-ups & Break-downs	285
131.	Pot in a Sock	289
132.	Size 13 Pep Talk	291
133.	What We remember about Certain Games	293
134.	A Second Chance	297
135.	Pre-Game Meal	299
136.	Rookie Plane Trip	301
137.	The Wrong Ronnie	303
138.	The Swimming Pool Incident	305

Table Of Contents

139.	Another Time	307
140.	"Give me an A!!"	309
141.	Dick Edell's Big Escape	311
142.	The "Left handed Face-off"	315
143.	Drinking the Wrong Beverages	319
144.	When the Twins were born	323
145.	The Power of the Aspirin	325
146.	Sometimes You Get the Bear	327
147.	A Blue Jay All the Way	329
148.	Always Check your Equipment	333
149.	Can You Hear Me in the Back	335
150.	Summer Camp Manager of the Year	337
151.	The Tail Gaters	339
152.	Parents with an Answer	341
153.	Similar Situation – Different Parents	343
154.	The Hospitalization of Dick Edell	347
155.	What Strange Creatures these Coaches Are	351
156.	A Cold Whirlpool	353
157.	A Young Man any Coach would love to have	355
158.	Friendly Consoling	357
159.	Kids Say the Darndest Things	361
160.	The Barbershoppers	363
161.	The Annual Police Department Picnic	365
162.	The Super Bowl Party	369
163.	Duffy	371
164.	If He Goes to Carolina … Leave Him!!!	373
165.	Keeping the Officials on Their Toes	375
166.	Still on their Toes!	377
167.	The New Van	379
168.	What did I do With That Kid	383
169.	Jerry Thelen	385
170.	Runk's Mountain	389
171.	Never Trust your Judgement	391
172.	The New Sports Jacket	393
173.	Applying the Pavlov Theory	395
174.	Andy Nelson	399
175.	Brenda	403

176. The Hole in One 405
177. Father Jim................................407

TOWSON STATE—First row, left to right: *Eisenhut, Darcangelo, Moore, Baldini, Griebe, Marshall, Russo, Jones, Levy, Dougherty, Nelson* Second row: *Ferrante, Hoge, Lekas, Chasney, Eichelberger, Cook, Thomas, Mollet, Kimball, Anderson, Bernstein;* Top row: *Head Coach Carl Runk, Sisson, B. Moore, Stein, McGarity, Lafferty, Monath, Miller, Maher, Harrison, Clarke, Youngman, Stratton, Assistant Coaches Hugh Mallon and Joe Ardolino.*

MEL FERNWACKER

SUBMITTED BY
CARL RUNK

In the early "70's I was fortunate enough to be selected to coach the South Team in the classic "North / South seniors lacrosse game, being held in Ithaca, New York at the prestige's Cornell University. Dick Edell, then the head coach at the United States Military Academy, was selected to coach the North. It was a time when this particular game received tremendous public exposure and was highly popular with the fans. The night before the big game, the senior players, both north and south, were honored by the city of Ithaca at a down town evening banquet. Besides the entourage of lacrosse affiliates and officials there was also the mayor of Ithaca along with city council members. After dinner, Richie Moran, long time successful coach at Cornell University, gathered Dick Edell and myself to a meeting informing us that we would have to go up on stage and introduce the players of our respective teams. I thought he was kidding but he was dead serious! "Richie, I said, you want me to introduce these players and I don't even know they're names!" "You've got about five minutes to learn em!" he responded. I had no idea how I was going to handle this situation and literally hit the panic button! Finally, an assistant coach informed me that I could use the banquet program which included the players' name, college, and position. Thank the Lord!! Here was a solution to a most possible embarrassing situation. Dick Edell was to go on stage first and introduce his team, which meant at this time, I could study the program and give the impression I knew what the hell I was talking about. With a new surge of confidence, I stood at the base of the stage ready to introduce my team when called on. In his closing remarks, Edell suddenly pays tribute to the team manager of the North squad, introducing him to the crowd! It was at this time I wanted to run up on stage and rip his heart out. Everything was going great until he did that! I had about 30 seconds to find out the name of our team manager and introduce him at the end of the player introductions. I quickly asked those around me the name of our manager, but no one knew. As I was introduced and walking up on stage I passed Edell. He was my last chance. "Rich, what's the name of my team manager?? He responded, "Oh, your team managers' name is Mel Fernwacker!" "Thanks, buddy, you saved the day!! After introducing my south squad I mentioned to the crowd "I would, at this time, like to introduce you to a young man who for the whole week has helped our squad above and beyond the call of duty. A devoted man, who catered to our every need. Ladies and gentlemen, the team manager of the south squad, Mr. Mel Fernwacker. Mel, would you please stand to be recognized!" Everyone in the banquet hall was looking around for Mel but no one stands up. "Mel, are you out there?" Finally, a young man in the back stands up and says, "Coach Runk!!" I went through hell this week….. Trying to get you everything you needed….. chewing tobacco…. special drinks… setting up the field for your secret practices in the pouring rain… and you don't even know my name!!!" Well, the crowd laughed unmercifully, and when I looked over to find Rich Edell, he was literally kneeling on the floor with his head in his hands, covered by a handkerchief, laughing his a_ _ off!!! For a person who thrives on kidding and fooling people I have never been so embarrassed in all my life. The big turkey really got me in front of all of those people!! And … I never got the chance to meet Mel Fernwacker!

THE NONPAREIL TRUFFLES

SUBMITTED BY
CARL RUNK

It was at the same contest, the North / South Classic at Cornell University that I made a game wager with Dick Edell. Back then coaches/teachers did not have the pleasure of a pay check coming in during the summer and had to find other part-time employment. My wife, Joan, & I opened a candy store in Ocean City, Maryland that was located right on the boardwalk. We literally sold the best chocolates in town! And, wouldn't you believe it....Dick Edell was one of our more frequent buyers! He really loved the cheaper costing candy. Just like today, he would never go deep into his pockets to buy the good stuff! Anyway.... the night before the game I told him if the South won the game he would have to give me a pair of Army shorts and tee-shirt. I thought he, being a Towson graduate, would opt for the Towson shorts and Tee shirt, though I knew we didn't have a pair of shorts big enough for his big a_ _ ! I completely forgot about his outrageous appetite for sweet (cheap) candies. He retorted, "I'll do it.....but only for a box of your best chocolates!" In my mind, there was no way we were going to lose. This seemed like a sure win!!

What I didn't take into consideration was the North's goalie, an athlete by the name of Rick Blick, from Hobart College. This youngster literally thrived on pain, a pure masochist! If he didn't have 15 or more welts on his body from shots after the game ended he would go into a deep depression, whether the team won or lost! Legend has it that Blick derived sensual pleasure by having lacrosse balls propelled at his rear end by a baseball pitching machine at a velocity of 75 miles an hour! (Obviously, that statement is not true! I just wanted to throw it in at this time!) We couldn't get a laser beam by Blick. He stopped everything we threw at him and then would give us hell for not shooting harder! Near the end of the 2nd quarter, with the score <u>North 10 – South 0</u>, I called a time out. As both teams huddled for instruction, I called Dick Edell to the middle of the field. "Rich", what kind of chocolates do you want??" He responded "I'd like a box of the nonpareil truffles in a dark chocolate!" I couldn't believe it!! He picked the most expensive chocolate I had!! I told him I would throw in an extra pound if he would bench Blick!! We still lost the game but were able to score a few in the second half. He benched Blick!! Later, I gave him a box of our best chocolates. I also went to the "Dollar Store" and picked up a box of "Whitman's" chocolates, placed them in one of our boxes and gave them to the big turkey. He didn't know the difference between a good chocolate and an "M & M!!" I don't think I'll ever forget that satisfied facial expression he displayed while eating those chocolates. Little did he know that they were "day olds" that I purchased at the dollar store with 50% off!!

FUN LOVING BLUE JAY

SUBMITTED BY
CARL RUNK

Before the benefit of technical support and filming contests, coaches, in scouting, would rely on observing the game and writing down information to be included in the scouting report. This could be accomplished a number of different ways. One of the ways, though it was strongly frowned on, was to stand right on the field at the back line behind the goal, either at the offensive end or the defensive end. And wouldn't you know, it was usually on the offensive end. We were playing at home when I recognized an opposing coach scouting our game from behind the offensive end of the field. Being a paranoid type coach, I called a time out and told our players what was taking place. The youngsters were informed that everything they said or did was being written down and diagramed. Since we were playing a less experienced team at the time and there was little chance of losing, our strategy was to call out a name, any name, hold the hand up in the air, and helter-skelter all over the place. We knew the opposing coach would copy all that information down. I would have loved to have seen the diagram or have been at his practice when he explained it to his kids in the scouting report.

Our youngsters were bringing the ball in bounds, calling out names like "fun loving blue jay" or "streaking tiger" and running all over the place. The opposing coach was writing as fast as he could. We really showed him! Two week later we were to play the scouting coach's team. While the game was going on, with the ball on our offensive end of the field, the opposing coach would call out, "Watch out for fun-loving blue jay!!" or "Be alert of streaking tiger!!". Our youngsters really enjoyed that game. A few weeks later, while scouting a school that would play this same team, with the score tied in the closing minute of the game, the coach calls out to his team <u>"run the fun-loving blue jay!!"</u> Would you believe they scored and won the game on the "fun loving blue-jay" call!!! That win placed him above us in the conference standings! Though he never gave us credit for it, he later showed the play (?) at a local offensive coaching clinic. So much for offensive strategy.

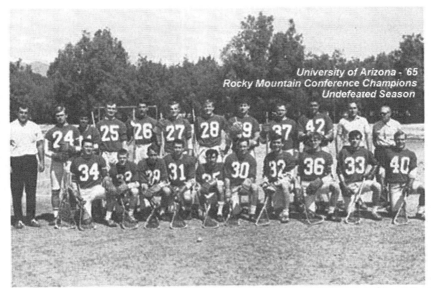

LACROSSE: Bottom Row: Tom Hippert, Seth Gibson, Dave Weaver, Lowell Copeland, Don Melhado, Cody Copeland, Van Seldon, Wally Sharts, Dick Smith, Dave Handschumacher, captain. Row II: Carl Runk Coach, Barry Bingen, Mick Graham, Neil Stroman, Jim Bruner, Brian Hogan, Tom Cookingham, Tim Colman, Lee Marshlow, Bob Badger, assistant coach, Willy Cooper, faculty advisor, John Anthony.

THE BANK REST STOP

SUBMITTED BY
CARL RUNK

Some of the most difficult times in my coaching career came while I was coaching the University of Arizona lacrosse teams during the "60's. The players were great to work with and a fantastic bunch of young men. The difficulty came with the travel to play contests. The closest game was Arizona State up at Tempe, which was 135 miles away. The next closest contest was at Los Angeles, California which was about 450 away. After that, mileage was based on hours. 22 hours to the Air Force Academy, and approximately 18 + hours to Salt Lake City Utah. The contests were always multi-team games, that is leaving Tucson early Thursday morning, playing the Air Force Academy on Friday, University of Colorado on Saturday, and Denver University at 9:00 am Sunday morning, leaving right after the game, hopefully before noon and heading home. The camaraderie was overwhelming. Because of the low allocated budgets, home teams were responsible for the housing and feeding of the visiting players. Without this kind of support it would have been impossible to have a full season of play. Funds for our travel meals were provided by the donations of local lacrosse enthusiasts and there weren't too many of them! Believe it or not, back then when you stopped to purchase gas you would receive "green stamps" which you placed in a book. The number of books you were able to accumulate over time determined the prizes you qualified for. I always made sure we would stop for gas at the stations that gave the stamps. It did make for a nice gift to my wife, Joan. With a caravan of 4 vehicles, station wagons, we would drive half a day, stop in a small town, to eat. I would go into a super market, buy the meat, cheese, condiments, several loafs of bread, and the soft drinks. The food was laid out on one of the station wagons with the meat, cheese, condiments and bread placed on the hood of the car, and the soft drinks placed on the back door which was laid down. The order was easy. Referred to as "circle the wagons", each player was to circle the car until all the food was gone and at that time, we loaded back up to finish the trip. It was on the return home trip from Boulder, Colorado, with the drivers very sleepy, that I signaled to stop at the next rest stop or town to take a 15/20 minute nap. We were coming into a small town in New Mexico, named "Truth or Consequences" about 3:00 am. Since there were no street lights everything was totally dark. I saw a large parking lot which I assumed was a supermarket and beckoned the other cars to park and take that nap. I'm not sure how long

The Bank Rest Stop

we slept but I do remember being prodded with a stick and being awakened by bright lights in my face. Each car was being questioned by the state police as to what our intentions were. I tried to explain we represented the University of Arizona, that we were on our way back to Tucson, when we decided to stop and take a nap. The police officers were confused and wanted to know what the hell we were going to use the sticks for. After trying to explain the sport of lacrosse, it was <u>overwhelmingly</u> decided that we should move on and stop at the rest stop out of town and a few miles away. As we departed from the lot, I could see from the large sign out front the building that we didn't stop at a shopping mart but had parked on the lot of the local bank. The officers actually thought we were going to rob the bank! Hell, I didn't need to rob a bank!! I was getting "green stamps!!"

KIDS WILL DO THE DARNDEST THINGS

SUBMITTED BY
CARL RUNK

One of the enjoyments I received from coaching was having the opportunity to have my son's Keith, Carl, & Curt travel with the team to away contests. To me, it was to be a positive and memorable experience for the boys, one that would contribute to the development of their attitude and values. Curtis, the youngest of the three, and approximately four years old, was blessed with an outstanding personality. In a crowd, he seemed to blossom as the central figure of discussion and entertainment. The players literally locked him in a locker while they dressed and prepared for practice. Another time I was called by the campus police to come to the student union immediately. They wanted direction as to how they should attempt to remove his arm from the coca-cola machine. Seems the youngster was coached by the players to put his whole arm up the vending machine and try to get free drinks. Unfortunately, he was unable to get the arm out, was caught and had to spend 40 years in jail....attached to the coke machine! Only Joking!!

We were on our way home from Delaware on a bus when Curt, in the back of the bus, started to yell, "Ohhh, that's bad!" "I'm going to tell my daddy!" I knew then that maybe bringing the boys on the bus was not a good idea, it didn't allow the players the verbal freedom they needed. Especially with Curtis around! He came down the aisle and started to yell to me that a player in the back made a bad sign with his finger. There are times, as a coach, when you don't want to acknowledge some things that the players do. This was one of those times. But the little "bugger" wouldn't stop until I addressed the situation. After finding out, by Curtis, who the culprit was, I told him I wanted to meet with him in my office when we got to Towson. I later was told by the player that he was talking with another player across the aisle and gave him the finger. He said he was unaware that the youngster was observing. I told him that Curt was a hearing impaired youngster and very observant. He, and the other player, would have to watch what they say or do when around the boy. He agreed and we left it at that. On the way out the gym, holding Curtis's hand with my right hand, we passed by the admissions director, Mike Mahoney and the player, Sam Pavaola, on my left, and bid each other good night. It was approximately 20 years later, at an alumni function that I met the player involved, Sam Pavoala and the admissions director, Mike Mahoney. As we talked about old times, Mike asked if I remembered that incident. I said I did. Mike asked if I remember coming out of the gym holding Curtis's hand and saying good night to them as they stood by. I replied that I did. Mike then told me as "you passed by us, holding Curt's left hand, your cute little boy took his free hand, placed it behind his back, where you could not see it, and gave us the finger!!" Now isn't that something!! Do you think this could have been an inherited trait from his mother's side?!

A TEACHING TECHNIQUE

SUBMITTED BY
CARL RUNK

A few years back I had the opportunity to speak at a coach's clinic in Syracuse, New York. My presentation involved the clearing game and how to approach it in practice. This was at a time when a lot of practice was spent on clearing and riding. Prior to the clinic I had an opportunity to visit with three of my ex-players who were coaching at the time and in attendance. I asked each one to sit in different areas of the arena. I also mentioned that I was going to call on each one at a certain time during my lecture, and ask them to tell me their responsibility on certain clears. At that time, I wanted them to stand up and without hesitation, yell out "Coach, on this clear I would start at the __ position and quickly move to the __ position!" I also gave each one an index card with a separate answer typed on it for them to read out.

While going through the presentation I tried to emphasize the importance of this phase of the game, how significant it was that the players know exactly what to do, and how quickly it could be incorporated into the practice schedule. I actually had clinic players available to demonstrate all the clears and showed how quickly these clears could be learned. I tried to emphasize to the coaches that it was worth the time, easy to do, and something they could easily remember. That it would stay with them. At this time, I called out asking if there were any ex-Towson players present. When the three hands went up I exclaimed to the crowd that I didn't know if they were here and that I wanted to prove a point. I called out to each ex-player, individually, to tell me exactly what they would do on the "mike" clear, or the "red d" clear, and on the "alley" clear. All three responded precisely as instructed and we literally knocked the crowd over. They were totally impressed with my technique and sold on my philosophy. Aint I something!!

Approximately 10 years later, Paul Werhum, successful coach of Herkimer Community College & Hall of Fame member, was speaking at a clinic. Paul was a highly emotional coach, a coach who thrived on inspiration, from those around him, from written or spoken statements, and was driven to create a positive environment within his team. As he spoke on his topic he paused for a moment to shed light on how impressed he was, years back, as he sat at a coaching clinic listening to "Coach Runk talk about his strategy in coaching"! He was highly impressed by the response of the ex-players that day, and how they, after all those years, still remembered their assignments! He said this was a coaching strategy, at that time, he himself must adopt and apply to his program. I never had the heart to tell Paul that I was just "Joshing" and that I struggled, just like any other coach, to get the "little pencil-necks" to do what I wanted! (half the time they never did!!) Paul, where ever you are……. I hope you won't feel ill towards me!

JUST DOING HIS JOB

SUBMITTED BY
CARL RUNK

The face-off has always been a beautiful part of lacrosse. I hope we never get to the time when the scored upon team will get possession of the ball after a score, just as we have in some other sports. I do, however, believe that within a short period time this will be just the case. As a lacrosse enthusiast I totally enjoy watching the specialist do their thing when facing off. However, with the growth of the game at the present time, and the overwhelming popularity, there may be a move to see certain phases of the game given a lesser role, one not so prominent.

It was an early season scrimmage contest against an up and coming Syracuse team. This contest was being played at Towson and was well attended. Syracuse was a "blue collar" team and we were well aware that it was to be a physically oriented game. Syracuse had one standout athlete, a pro-prospect football player who enjoyed knocking the heck out of the opposition on loose ball plays. He was especially aggressive on the face-off. At that period of time, a wing midfielder could play havoc on the opposing teams' face-off man. This individual did just that.

He would constantly inflict pain on our little draw man. It was to the point where I wanted to see him get stuck. We called a time out and in the huddle I informed the team of my strategy. "Get 'em back" time! Joe Ferrante, a hard nose player who would run through a wall for you, if you showed him which wall, was the designated assassin. I told Joe, on the face-off, I wanted him to concentrate solely on the football player, not even to worry about the ball. His mission was to "knock the hell" out of the big bugger!! He was to sacrifice his body for the sake of the team. As they lined up for the face-off, the intensity was overwhelming. Our heat seeking missile, Joe Ferrante, was ready to be launched. The whistle blew and both teams converged to the middle. Then, because of an infraction, there was a second whistle to stop play. Everyone stopped, relaxed, and looked at the official…….except Joe!! Zeroed in on his target, he just kept coming. The scene resembled something out of a race car crash. The big relaxed football player got hit with a heck-of-a shot, and came up from the ground furious, trying to get at Joe. The official, Ron O'Leary, was angrier than the inflicted player. He grabbed Joe and shouted "he's got a minute for unsportsmanlike conduct!" With my quick thinking ability, I shouted to O'Leary "Ron, he didn't mean it………He's deaf, he can't hear the whistle!!" Ronnie looked back and responded, "Yeah, he's deaf…..but he's not that dumb!!"

WHOSE GOT # 24

SUBMITTED BY
CARL RUNK

How many times in coaching has the wrong message been sent at the most inappropriate time. We've all experienced this in one way or another. With the team up by a goal or two, and little time on the clock, the coach calls a time out to make sure every player understands the situation. After a thorough explanation, the players take the field and execute something that has never been seen before! The most embarrassing thing is convincing the spectators later that what the youngsters ran in the game was not what was discussed in the timeout. The following are examples of this scenario.

In a hard fought game against the United States Naval Academy a few years ago, with a minute left and the score tied, I called a time-out to organize the team as to how we would defense this group. We knew Navy would go with their best offensive threat and we decided to force them out of their offense, somewhat, by running a zone. I explicitly went over the zone we would run and felt confident it would confuse them. As we broke the huddle, the players ran to the field to take their position. One of our defenders, unfortunately something of an "air head", was shouting very loudly, " I've got number 24!!!" I knew then we were in a lot of trouble. It was a very long bus ride back home!

ANOTHER TIME

SUBMITTED BY
CARL RUNK

It was during the NCAA semi-finals a few years back. We had a great bunch of talented youngsters and were playing Maryland. If we win the contest we play in the Finals. It was a very exciting time. The clock showed approximately three minutes remaining with Towson leading by three goals. We were bringing the ball inbounds on the offensive end, from inside the restraining line, in a dead ball situation. Trying to look like I knew what the heck I was doing, I called a time out. In the huddle, I explained to the players we wanted to hold onto the ball, force Maryland to come after us, either with a single defender or with the double, and possibly foul us in the process. This would give us the one minute EMO cushion and, if we didn't screw things up, we would be going to the Finals! The player bringing the ball inbounds was a very competent lacrosse player but, unfortunately, mentally similar to the defender "who had number 24!!" At the sound of the whistle, he drove straight to the goal and shot the ball ... perfectly into the goalie's stick. I have never experienced a desire to physically correct a player like I did for this youngster at that time! I could have rung his neck!! Fortunately, we had a group of young men who responded to the adversity in a positive manner. We finally won the game.

I did, however, also benefit from this ordeal, to a great extent, through my monthly visits to my cardiologist!

LIKE YOU FELL OUT OF A PLANE

SUBMITTED BY
CARL RUNK

One of the rewards of coaching is having the opportunity to see young people experience various circumstances of adversity, and to have them grow in a positive manner from that situation. We, confidently, anticipate a life learning lesson, either good or bad, that might assist in the character development of these players.

    I recall one of those opportunities a few years back. We were playing a very good Johns Hopkins team at home, in the evening. In order for our team to be successful everything had to be right. That is, we had to play the percentage game; control the face-offs, slow the ball down, take high percentage shots, no fouls, get the ground balls, strong defense, and, among other things, our stopper had to have the game of his life! It could be done! Our game plan was simple. If we could stay close for three quarters, our momentum would carry us through the fourth. Also in our favor was the crowd. The stadium was packed and they were looking forward to a great game. That's exactly what the kids gave them. Any time we played Hopkins our youngsters played extremely hard. Late in the fourth quarter, in a very close game, the momentum seemed to drift towards the blue jays. I was becoming frustrated with our kids, as were my assistant coaches, Joe Ardolino and Jeff Clarke. Both coaches came to me yelling "coach, we're losing it. We have to get the kids back on track!!" "Call a time-out!" I was very upset at the turn of events and I totally agreed with both Joe and Jeff. I called for a time out and started to walk out on the field. This was a super opportunity for the players to experience character development through coaching brutality. As we walked to the center of the field, Joe starts to bear to the right and calls for all the offensive players to huddle around him. Jeff bears to the left and calls for all the defenders. I am standing in the middle of the field, like I fell out of a plane, with no one around me but a short, chunky, third string goalie with his hand in a cast, waiting for me to give some kind of worldly advise about having pride or character or something like that!! I felt like I had every eye in the stadium on me at that time. That was a highly embarrassing moment! I looked down into the round, inquisitive blue eyes of the rotund goalie and said "Son, if you walk away from me now, you'll never play lacrosse again in your life!! I often wonder if that player learned any "life saving" experience at that time. I sure in hell did!! That was the last time we went to offensive and defensive huddles!

LEARNING FROM THE EXPERIENCED

SUBMITTED BY
CARL RUNK

The growth of lacrosse has improved immensely. The numbers of players participating is overwhelmingly high and the technique used by these youngsters is better than ever before. Coaches are more learned and able to instruct at a higher level. This, I believe, can be attributed to the advancement of individual and team technique, along with the game strategies that have been made available to the coaches through local and national clinics. This was not always the case, though! I attended my first lacrosse clinic up in Long Island, New York in 1967. It was my first year as the head coach of Towson University, then known as Towson College. The opportunity to get out and meet new coaches in the game was very appealing to me.

The clinic, held in a small dining room at a local restaurant, was none to impressive. There were about 6 rows of chairs, approximately 8 chairs per row. Every coach was dressed in either a sport coat or suit, with a tie. Everyone sat at attention, in a military manner, and displayed a quiet demeanor. After a period of time, I felt like I was at a funeral and occasionally would give my condolences and sympathy to a participating member. It was, without a doubt, the most boring ordeal I have ever been through. The clinicians were gifted with the ability to put any or all coaches present into a deep trance in no time flat! <u>And they did!</u> If you have ever listened to Richie Moran, lacrosse Hall of Famer, you know what I mean. (Only kidding, Rich) I was asked by a soon-to-pass-on coach to promise him, before he went to the big lacrosse field in the sky, I would take an oath, at that time, if I ever had the opportunity to speak at a clinic, I would do everything possible not to let anyone experience what he was forced to endure that day. "If it sounds a little exaggerated…..it is!!" But that's how boring it was.

I, fortunately, was seated in the last row and second from last seat. The last seat was occupied by a handsome, silver haired gentleman, by the name of Roy Simmons Sr., the father of the very successful long time Syracuse coach, Roy Simmons Jr. Coach Simmons was the head lacrosse coach at Syracuse and was also an assistant football coach. Being the newly appointed football coach at Towson, I had the opportunity to gain a wealth of knowledge about the game of football and I did! It seems Coach Simmons was just as bored as I was and agreed to let me pick his brain. We just sat in the back and exchanged ideas and notes regarding offensive and defensive technique & schemes. He was very kind and considerate to a young and aspiring coach that day and probably didn't recognize the positive impression he had made. When I arrived back to Towson I was asked by my athletic director if I had a good experience at the clinic. Without hesitation, I responded yes, I had learned a great deal and definitely would put those lessons to use.

THE STARTING PISTOL

SUBMITTED BY
CARL RUNK

I always enjoyed being on the clinic agenda and was impressed with the aggressiveness of the ccaches in our game. By that, I simply mean they were really into the improvement of the individual player, team, and game concepts. These were not "rent a coach" type people, doing it just for the stipend. (which was/is minimal anyway!) They truthfully enjoyed the game and contributing to it. Like all coaches, the sense of humor was overwhelming. They loved a good story or prank. I had the occasion to speak at the Long Island Coaches Clinic years back. I really enjoyed doing this as it gave me the exposure I needed for my school, helped recruiting, and, last but not least, it gave me the opportunity to be with old friends. Before my presentation, I met with an old friend, Fran McCall, who was known by every coach in the game. Fran was a great coach, at Bethpage High School, but, above all, a beautiful person. We had great times together. As we sat and talked, I told Fran of my plans for the presentation and asked if he would assist at a certain time. He enthusiastically accepted. I can't recall the topic but remember at the end of the talk trying to emphasize to the audience the importance of commitment and not letting anything get in your way. I then asked if there were any questions or concerns I might cover. At that time, Fran, who was strategically seated in the front row, jumped up and exclaimed, "Carl, I've been sitting here for the past hour listening to you and I still do not understand a thing you've said!!" I stepped to the side of the podium, reached inside my sport coat and brought out a pistol. I quickly pointed it at Fran and fired a whopper of a shot! The blast from that shot was loud and scared the heck out of all the coaches. Fran fell back into his seat slumping over. I very calmly blew the smoke from the gun and retorted "Are there any other questions??!!"

It's amazing all the attention you can get with a "starting" pistol and blanks!!

THE STYROFOAM BRICKS

SUBMITTED BY
CARL RUNK

At another time I was asked to give a presentation at a clinic.

In preparing, I had asked my wife Joan, when going to the shopping center, to pick up a couple pieces of sponge rubber, or Styrofoam about the size of a brick, which she did. I took the two pieces of sponge rubber, along with two regular bricks and painted all four red. I later traveled to Long Island to the coach's clinic where I was presenting. During the presentation, I emphasized the importance of getting the players' attention, and how vital it was. I told the story of the zoo keeper with the bricks. He was asked why he kept them. "Sometimes the elephants won't listen and in order to get their attention I must go around back, lift up their tale and, with a brick in both hands, slam the bricks together on the elephant's gonads!! Now they will listen to me!" As I told the story, I would emphasize getting the players' attention by slamming the bricks together. What they didn't know, at the end of the presentation, I put the real bricks down and picked up the sponge rubber bricks that looked the same. With a brick in both hands, I mentioned, one more time, the importance of "getting their attention" and then I said "just like I'm going to get yours!!" I reached back in a baseball pitcher stance and threw both bricks into the audience. Those surprised coaches scattered out of the seats like someone called out "Free Beer!!" I never saw a bunch of guys move as quickly as they did!! It was my turn! I really got them!! Would you believe, later in the week, I got a call from one of the coaches, telling me he was going to speak to a group and wanted to know if he could borrow my bricks!!

COACHING YOUR OWN

SUBMITTED BY
CARL RUNK

I would only hope every coach could have the opportunity to have his own youngsters on his team. I have been very fortunate to have coached my sons, Keith, Carl, and Curt in wrestling and that was a special time. It was also special to have Keith as a member of my Towson lacrosse team. I cherish the memories of the practices, games, trips, and the rides home just talking and sharing thoughts with him. Keith was a good athlete and played the position of goalie. He probably could have started for a large number of schools but he chose Towson at a time when we had one of the best in the game. I was glad he did. He was great to have on the team and never once did he tarnish his loyalty to his teammates by bringing stories home, probably because he was involved with the stories. He was a true teammate! He would laugh so very hard at the dinner table as both his mother and grandmother would run me through the mill wanting me to justify why he wasn't starting or playing more. There were times when I just wanted to drop him off at the house and keep going! Those were very special years for me.

I remember sitting at the dinner table years later discussing personnel with my wife, Joan. I mentioned one of the players, in particular, because his parents and Joan & I had grown up together. We were good friends. The youngster, an outstanding player in high school, was highly independent and prone to do his own thing. In contrast, we had our own philosophy about how things were to be accomplished. Bottom line … do it our way or sit the bench! I told Joan I was concerned about our relationship with the parents. I said we may lose our friendship with the couple because of their love and loyalty to their son. I said, "You know, blood runs thicker than water!" Having said that, my wife Joan jumped up from the dinner table and exclaimed in a loud voice "That's all bull crap!! I <u>slept</u> with my son's coach for <u>four years</u> and <u>he</u> didn't play!!! I don't want to hear about blood and water!!"

MY OLD FRIEND DANNY

SUBMITTED BY
CARL RUNK

I have been asked numerous times as to what have been my proudest moments in this great game. Though I have been fortunate to have a few, one seems to always take a front and center position. During his playing days, Danny Nolan was a big dominating type midfielder who gave us outstanding support and our player's tremendous confidence in our style of play. He was a solid competitor and I was glad he was with us. After graduation Danny assisted at Towson in a coaching capacity for about one year. He was named head lacrosse coach at the Christ Church School in Christ Church, Virginia and later was appointed athletic director at the same school. It was at this time that Danny was diagnosed with "Lou Gehrig's disease. Though he fought this disease with every competitive fiber in his body, his physical condition became progressively worse. Danny succumbed to this tragic disease on March 9th, 1992. I don't ever think of Danny without receiving an overwhelming feeling of warmth, comfort, and peace of mind.

During the '91 quarter finals in Charlottesville, Virginia, with Towson, ranked 11th or 12th , about to play the

University of Virginia, I met Danny just outside the locker rooms. With Danny in his newly acquired wheel chair, we were able to cross the field and let him view the game from the sidelines. We won the contest and I recall Danny telling me he couldn't make the next game but would surely be at the finals. I told him if we made the finals he would be on the sideline with us. With an inspired bunch of young men, we made it to the finals!

The NCAA administrative meeting, to cover the protocol of the event, is usually held the day before the championship game. Present at this meeting were the administrative members representing both schools, the coaches, and the NCAA representatives. All areas of this spectacular were covered and at the end of the meetings the NCAA representatives asked if we, the coaches, had anything to add. I said I had a concern. It involved bringing "one of our people" who was in a wheel chair, on the field, specifically to our sideline. I was quickly informed that this could not be accomplished and that there was an area, for wheelchairs only, in the dome. For some unknown reason, I recall looking the administrator straight in the eye and exclaiming, "then I hope you are totally aware that you are in violation of Public Law 94-142, the public law protecting the disabled!" (It should be noted here that I was very up to date on the benefits of the disabled because of my graduate work at Gallaudet College, a college for the deaf.) There was a pause of silence for what seemed an eternity. I, then, thought to myself "Why the hell did you say that!! At that point one administrator looked to a co-administrator and said, "You know… I don't see any problem with having this person on the sidelines, do you?" <u>Bingo!!</u> It was agreed Danny could view the games from our sidelines but must be out of the way of the players on the field.

As our players were taking the field for pre-game warm-ups, I went to the players' entrance of the dome. Danny was there waiting for the large double gate door to open. As gate opened we both entered the dome, walking diagonally across the field to our sideline, I don't think I have ever been any prouder than that moment.

    Pleasant memories of an old friend.

OLD BUCK TAYLOR

SUBMITTED BY
CARL RUNK

Throughout my young adult life in athletics, specifically football, I had always been brainwashed by coaches at the junior league, high school, and college level how important it was, when tackling an opponent, to "use your head!" How many times did I hear the phrase "Bull your neck, stick your face in there! It aint gonna hurt you!" More than I wanted. It seemed like the most important ingredient to becoming an outstanding player. "He's a great player..... He aint afraid to stick his face in there!!" I was fortunate to grow up with a tremendous bunch of guys. We were also group oriented. A bunch of guys, all about the same age, living in the same neighborhood in east Baltimore. We would congregate at various places, especially the park." Since there was no television back then and none of us were interested in reading books, we spent many days in the park playing ball.

Quite often, in the park, we would have "two hand touch" football games within our own group. There were some extremely tough games that we played but it was a great experience. Occasionally we would challenge or be challenged by another local gang to participate in a tackle football contest. The attire was simple. There would be no pads worn by any member of either team. However, a player could wear football shoes if, he had them. This inter-neighborhood contest would have a specific time and place, usually the park on a Saturday morning. As fate would have it, we scouted a group from an area called "Canton" and it was decided we could beat them in a game of football thus improving our image and credentials. It was all set. Saturday, at 11:00 a.m., in the park. Little did we know that the opposition would have a "ringer" on their team! ("Ringer" is a term used when a team involves a player who is older, bigger, and/or stronger than all other players.) This is usually a frowned on practice. The day of the contest we were stunned to see the "Ringer". It was Buck Taylor! He was the only 16 year old in America who had the physique of a body builder and looked like he was 40 years old! He had more hair on his chest than 3 of us had on our head!! As you very well know, there is a big difference physically between a fourteen year old and a sixteen year old. We all knew it but didn't have the courage to tell Buck he couldn't play.

Our strategy was simple.....Keep the ball away from Buck on the kick-off. And wouldn't you know it.....I kicked the ball right to him! As we were running down the field I could hear the guys yelling at me calling "you dumb ass.....you kicked it right to Buck!!" There wasn't anything fancy about that big hombre. He just ran straight ahead like a Brahma bull, destroying anything in front of him. On the kick-off, one of our gallant players dove from the side and caught Buck by the trousers, literally tearing the front of his pants off, fly and everything. Buck was now running totally exposed with his massive equipment swinging from side to side. I was amazed at his development. At that immediate time I thought to myself, "Holy Cripe, this guy is enormous!! Then I thought "why him and not me?!! Was I neglected in life or did I have this to look forward to when I turned 16!!!"

As fate would have it, he had only one person to beat to go all the way. Me!! It was going to be a head on collision. In life we're called on to make certain decisions that will stay with us throughout our time. All I could think of was the coaches in my formative years telling me to "Bull your neck and put your head right in there. Don't be a sissy!! Buck and his equipment were coming right at me. There was nothing deceptive about his run. It was time for me to make that decision! It was a moment when I was called to task. When I could have gained total respect from my peers!

Unfortunately, we lost that game 6 to 0!! Aint <u>no way</u> I was going to use the technique the coaches stressed all the time! I guess I looked just like a traffic cop at the time Buck passed me by! The other players on my team were really upset with me! Didn't talk to me for the rest of the day!! To this day I wonder "what the hell the other players on my team would have done if they were in my position!" I've always regretted the loss but have never given second thought to my decision!!

And I never caught up to Buck physically when I turned sixteen.

A GIFT FROM WILLIE COOPER

SUBMITTED BY
CARL RUNK

As head coach of the Arizona University lacrosse team I was fortunate to have coached many outstanding young men. I was very young at the time also, 24ish, and really enjoyed my position. An outstanding young athlete, Willie Cooper, played the midfield position and was very prominent in our success. After graduation Willie stayed on and assisted as a coach while he worked in graduate school. We were very successful in my last year at Arizona going 11 and 0, undefeated, which included two victories over the Air Force Academy. Quite an accomplishment for our team!

It was at that time I was contacted by Towson University to accept the head coaching position at that institution, which I did. One of the more difficult things we have to do when changing positions in coaching is to say goodbye to your team. This was one of those times. Willie Cooper, one of the most brilliant individuals I have ever known and presently a well- known nuclear physicist, who has spent most of his life experimenting with advanced explosives, came to me to wish me well in my new coaching venture. He said he was sorry to have me leave but wished me success in the future. He handed me a gift package he wanted me to have. The package contained an object that was quite different from anything I had ever seen before. It was a metal pyramid shaped object about 6 inches high and 6 inches at the base. The front was covered with little blue lights, one at the top, two in the second row, three in the third row, (you're getting the picture!) increasing with each row until reaching the final row which numbered about twenty lights . My response was one of gratitude, and it was something I would always cherish but I had to ask him one question. "What the hell is it?" He said it was a conversation piece. He had designed the lights to blink one at a time, constantly changing, and never duplicating a pattern. "Never in your lifetime!!" "Just place it on the living room mantle and when you have company it will help initiate conversation!" I must say I was really overwhelmed. He literally made this no-name blinking metal pyramid object for me! This was something very special and I would never part from it. Enter Joan!! (my wife) I couldn't wait to get home and surprise Joan with my newly acquired gift. At home, I quickly went to the living room, placed the pyramid on the mantle, and sat in my easy chair staring at this fascinating object. Joan entered the room and noticed it immediately. "What the hell is that?? I quickly responded, in a knowingly manner, that it was a gift from Willie, a conversation piece. "He designed it so it would never show a duplicate pattern in the blinking system." Joan retorted in a very disciplined manner "I don't care what the hell it does, just get it the hell off of my mantle!!"

Sometimes I just don't understand that woman and her lack of respect for worldly things. However, in passing years, the pyramid has been a comfort to our family and friends in its new site … you guessed it!

And wouldn't you know, it is quite remarkable how a metal object can be so soothing, comforting, and therapeutic if placed in the proper environment.

OLD BUCK

SUBMITTED BY
CARL RUNK

I remember having one of those periods of time where nothing seems to go right! We had lost the ball game the previous week-end, Sunday's film preview of the next opponent was not encouraging, and practice on Monday was for the dogs. During my ride home after practice I remember contemplating how things were going to change and I would be the person who would lead the charge. I would not allow these depressing episodes get me down. From this point on my attitude would be of a very positive nature. Most importantly, the reflection of my pro-active demeanor would rub off on all those around me. I really started to feel good about the situation. Make a positive out of a negative!

As I pulled up to my house I saw my black lab, Buck, sitting out on the pavement looking up to the front door, which was up a short hill, about 20 yards away. My first thought was "what the hell is he doing out here!! It is important to state at this time that Buck was the most intelligent dog we had ever owned and he had a mind of his own. Any time he got out by himself... <u>he was gone</u>!!!

Most likely looking for an area where he could lower his testosterone level. I yelled to get his attention and when I reached out to grab his collar, he snapped at me. I smacked him across the head yelling "Don't you ever snap at me!" That dog fought me all the way up to the door, growling, resisting, and snapping, being meaner than I've ever seen him before. Despite all his resistance, I was determined to show him who was boss. Every time he snapped at me I slapped him across the head. In a bent over position, eye level with this pissed-off pooch, I approached and opened the storm door. I then grabbed the main door knob to get inside. It was at this time a very strange thing happened. I glanced through the glass frame of the main door and saw my dog Buck just sitting there on the other side of that door observing everything that was taking place. I immediately turned back and looked at this creature I had been fighting for the past 5 minutes with his snarling features. His lip was up above his nose, exposing about an inch and a half of ugly gums, and his teeth, especially his fangs, were dripping with a thick coating of saliva! Holy crap!! If you know anything about coaching, this was the perfect time to initiate the <u>two minute drill</u>!!! How the hell was I going to get into the house without sharing my ass with this monster? He snapped, I slapped and opened the door at the same time, diving safely inside. As I turned around to look out the door, the dog I thought was mine, turned in an arrogant manner, marked his territory by urinating on my railing and proudly strutted down the street.

REMEMBERING THE "LORDS" PRAYER

SUBMITTED BY
CARL RUNK

My first assignment in coaching was at a high school in Tucson, Arizona. I was appointed to assist in football and to be the head wrestling coach. This was an important time for me to express my philosophy and techniques to highly enthusiastic young men. It was a time when I possibly could be a positive influence on these growing athletes. We worked very hard in the wrestling program as the majority of the members were in-experienced, as was their coach.

The time came for our first match which was a three-team tournament. We would finally get a chance to see how far along we were and above all to see how far we had to go. I can remember the adrenaline flowing during the bus ride, weigh-in and the start of the matches. I wanted to assemble our team in a quite area where I could give some profound advice and instruction to build onto our confidence. (That's what coaches do!!) As the other coaches were trying to do the same thing, I found an area where we could meet as a team before the start of the matches.

It was in a small stairwell hallway where we finally got together. A confined area, quite dark, with only a brief amount of light coming through a small window on the door. As we gathered closely together, I told the wrestlers that I always found comfort in saying a little prayer before competition. Not that we win, but that the Lord give us the strength to participate to the best of our ability and that we be protected from injury. I said I would like to continue this practice and then asked that our group kneel so we could say a prayer. The team was in total agreement and we did kneel as a group. I thought to myself "this is great, I will start the Lord's prayer, and the others would join in!" I started the prayer. "Our Father, who art in heaven" and at that point I realized that I was the only one praying! I became overwhelmingly nervous solely because I expected everyone to pray but it just didn't happen. And would you believe, under these conditions, I completely forgot the rest of the words to the Lord's prayer!! I wasn't getting any support from the kids! I didn't know what to do. I only knew I would have to fake it. I lowered my head, proceeded to <u>mumble</u> which resulted in the destruction of the english language. I'll never forget our heavyweight, a big highly religious Mormon youth, lifting his head, turning to look me straight in the eyes, trying to figure out what the hell was going on! At that point, I became so nervous I shouted out <u>"Let's go Gettum!"</u> The whole crowd jumped up and started cheering. I was totally embarrassed and as we returned to the gym going to our bench, I heard one of the kids exclaim "I like Coach. He's religious!" Another wrestler answered very quickly "Yeah and he speaks in tongues!"

TAKE OFF TODAY

SUBMITTED BY
CARL RUNK

If you have ever been involved with coaching, one thing is evident; you never forget your kids or what they mean to you. This has always been true especially in my situation with my wrestling team at Amphitheater High School, in Tucson, Arizona. How fortunate I was to have been associated with this fine group of young men. They totally believed in me and what we were trying to accomplish. I received an outstanding effort from the team every day. I would like to share a story about what kind of individuals I had on this team.

Our practice schedule was structured with certain drills being accomplished at various times during the two hour practice. In the early part of the week, we would send the youngsters out for a three mile run somewhere in the community. It was on a Monday and the team left the gym for the run. I would usually stay back, clean the mats and prepare for practice. This particular day the kids didn't return when they were supposed to. They were about ½ hour late and I didn't have a clue where they were.

When they finally arrived they were escorted by a few police officers. The wrestlers looked a little banged up and disarrayed physically. As fate would have it, as they ran north, they came into contact with a rival wrestling team, running south, on the same agenda when words were exchanged. The words lead to a physical confrontation with both teams fighting in the street. I asked the officers to please let me handle this situation. "I guarantee you I will reprimand the youngsters in a stern manner and you won't have to worry about this kind of conduct occurring again!" The officers agreed to the terms and left. I was extremely livid! "Who the hell do you think you are?!! You represent not only our team but also our school, and this community!" I will not stand for any embarrassing situations like this again. You can turn in your gear if it happens!" I continued to rant and rave but I remember ending by asking the kids "What do you think I'm doing this for? For the money?!!" "No way!! I'm not doing it for the money! I only make $.17 cents an hour working with you guys!!" I then proceeded to work these kids physically, harder than I have ever worked them before. It was the roughest practice we had been through during the entire season. When I arrived home that evening my wife, Joan, asked me how my day went. I told her about the episode at practice and how I was unbearably rough on the youngsters. I said, "I think I'll lose half of my kids, if not all of them, because of the way I worked them today. They were wrong but they didn't deserve that kind of physical punishment. We'll see tomorrow!!" The next day at the beginning of practice, the whole team was seated along the wall. I came into the room, which was unusually quiet. As I stepped onto the mat, the captains asked to see me. They both came to the center of the mat and said "Coach, we're sorry about yesterday. "We were wrong!! We want you to have this!!" They then handed me a quarter and a dime and told me to "Take off today! We'll handle practice ourselves!!" This attitude broke me up. I started to laugh and gave both wrestlers a big hug. Would you believe we had the best upbeat practice a coach could ask for.

As coaches, we are sometimes blessed to be associated with outstanding young people.

HOW TO STRENGTHEN YOUR WRIST

SUBMITTED BY
CARL RUNK

I was fortunate in my early coaching career to be mentored by some outstanding young coaches. Bobby Hart, my life-long friend, was one of those people. He was fun to be around and made you enjoy your day. When it came to coaching, he epitomized the best. Bobby was an offensive & defensive back coach in football during the fall of the year, officiated college basketball in the winter, and was the head baseball coach in the spring. He was one of the most dedicated coaches I've known. His week-ends were usually taken up with him being at the school pampering that baseball field. It wasn't unusual to see Bobby working the pitching mound while his wife would be pulling weeds in the outfield. He took tremendous pride in his assignments.

Bobby and I were sitting in our office discussing the benefits of weight training for athletes and the difference between baseball and lacrosse conditioning. My desk was along the wall and Bobby's was next to mine, near the door. It was at that time when one of the athletes came walking in the door. This youngster, without a doubt, was one of the best athletes in school. I wasn't too friendly with the player but that was only because he wouldn't come out for my wrestling team! His only reason to come in the office was to be pampered by his coach, Bobby. He was the kind of kid that wanted to hear about how great he was. He surely wouldn't hear it from me. The youngster, a top pitcher on the team, started to tell Bobby how anxious he was for the baseball season to start. He then asked Bobby "What can I do, Coach, to build up my wrists?" At this time, I was waiting for a highly intelligent response from my buddy, something on the scientific level. I was about to find out what they do in baseball. Without hesitating, while continuing to work on his workout schedule, he looked up and said "Lock your bathroom door!! The youngster looked at Bob with the strangest expression on his face. I almost fell on the floor! I thought that was one of the funniest things I'd ever heard. And would you believe to this day, when a youngster approaches me and asks "Coach, how can I improve my stickwork?!!," I think of my old friend Bobby and what he would tell them.

WHERE IS COACH HART

SUBMITTED BY
CARL RUNK

My close and dearest friend, Bobby Hart, recently reminded me of this episode that took place while I taught with him at the Amphitheater High School in Tucson Arizona. It sure brought back old memories.

I was sitting at my desk working on my lesson plan and directly behind me was the bathroom which was occupied by Bobby who was in the process of relieving himself. The bathroom door was closed. At this time, a very hyper and excited youngster came into the office wanting to know where Coach Hart was! "I have to see him immediately!! He has to sign these forms for me or I won't get my senior classes this semester. Do you know where he is? I really need to see him!" I casually responded and pointed to the bathroom door, "Yeah…he's in his office!!" The youngster walked quickly to the bathroom door and proceeded to walk in. Keep in mind…..the bathroom was not a big place but rather small. Bobby, quite surprised, standing with one hand bracing himself on the wall, and the other hand, having the responsibility of bathroom etiquette & accuracy, seemed a little upset! The youngster, not even aware of his surroundings, held the forms in front of Bobby's face and exclaimed, "Coach Hart, can you sign these forms for me? I've got to have them signed right now!" To which Bobby, somewhat irritated, sarcastically and quickly responded.. "Son, you hold this for me and I'll sign those damn papers right away!!"

Bobby then yelled to me, "Runk, I'll get you back for this!! I don't know when but I will!!" It was at that time that our department formulated a policy which made it compulsory for anyone using the bathroom to LOCK THE DOOR from the inside… This new rule seem to fit right into our comfort zone! Great memories!

BIG BAD JOHN

SUBMITTED BY
CARL RUNK

Jimmy Sandusky was a handsome young man and a good solid football player. He was the kind of person a parent would have loved and trusted to date their daughter. I liked him a lot but didn't trust him that much. I was fortunate to recruit him to Towson in my early years as the head football coach. Jim's dad was a well-known All Pro football player in his day for the Baltimore Colts and at that time the offensive line coach for that team. "Big John" is what the kid's referred to him as.

As I recall, we were playing a team in the lower part of Virginia on a Saturday afternoon and were en-route to this contest late Friday afternoon. It should be explained that the coaches, at that time, were responsible for the set-ups & break-downs for away games. This included travel, meals, and lodging. With a three man coaching staff, everyone was delegated a responsibility. I was responsible for the finances. My good friend, Phil Albert, was to take care of the players, which included roll call, room assignments and time schedules. Rich Bader was responsible for the amenities including where we would stop to eat. We

Along The Way

were so organized!! We stopped that evening at a Truck stop and I must say not one of the better ones! The truckers weren't the most congenial people you'd want to eat with and we had some verbal altercations during that time. I felt more like a traffic patrolman than a coach. After a short period of time we were back on the bus preparing to leave. I asked Coach Albert were all the players accounted for and he told me "we are ready to go". Arriving late at our destination, the players were given their room assignments and told that "lights out" would be 11:00 pm. Coach Albert was going around making sure everyone was in their room. He came back to the room and with that pale facial expression I'll never forget, exclaimed "Coach, we can't find Sandusky," He is nowhere to be found!" I asked, "Phil, are you sure?" His response was "Coach, he's not here!" My immediate thought was we left him at the truckstop and the truckers got him. I got on the phone to the truck stop and asked the manager if he could page "Jim Sandusky". I could hear the announcement on the loud speaker. The manager came back on line and told me there was no response but they would continue to look around and immediately call me if he turned up. After exhausting all possibilities, we came to the sorry conclusion that we would have to call the parents to tell them <u>we had lost their son!!</u> How the hell do you tell a 6'3" 300 lb + All Pro football player "Coach, would you ask Mrs. Sandusky to please set down"… and then proceed to tell them "we lost your son!!!"

    These were difficult times to say the least. I told Coach Albert to get the family phone number, call "Big John" and try to explain just what happened. "<u>We lost your son but we didn't mean to</u>!!!" Though coaches are supposed to be loyal and obedient to the head coach, Albert quickly refused and stated "something this serious demands a call from the head coach!" (damn sissy!) I reluctantly dialed that number and who do you think answered the phone? "Big John!!" "Coach" I said, "We've got a problem concerning Jimmy!" Before I could say anything else he jumped in and exclaimed,

"Coach Runk, I want you to know I'm really upset with that boy!! Who the hell does he think he is that he would stay home to go to a dance, of all things, instead of being with his team to play a game!! He's got a hell of a nerve!!" Hearing that statement, I quickly interrupted and said, "Coach, that's exactly what I want to talk about!!" "I am calling to tell you I won't tolerate that kind of behavior from anyone on our team!!" If it happens again, you can tell Jim he can go to all the dances he wants to! "We take tremendous pride in our program and want all our kids to do the same!!" "And you tell that pencil neck I can't wait to see him at practice on Monday!!"

Quick thinker aint I!!?

ST. PATRICKS' DAY GAME

SUBMITTED BY
CARL RUNK

I can truthfully say that in all the years of coaching lacrosse I never lost a game because of the officiating. There have been times when the calls didn't seem to go in my direction and I would be a little bent out of shape because of certain calls at inappropriate times, but throughout my tenure the officials did what they were supposed to do, call the game as best they could in an unbiased manner. We were playing at the University of Maryland unfortunately on St. Patrick's Day. This was an important game to our team. It would have definitely helped us in making the play-offs along with improving our recruiting program. Most of all, I just wanted to win the game.

We were on the field at Byrd Stadium early trying to acclimate as soon as possible, getting a good feel for the turf. Our warm-up intensified quite a bit when the Maryland team came out. You could feel the tension building up. It was at about 20 minutes before the contest when the two officials took the field coming over to our side first. At this time, we would usually go over field concerns, markings, equipment, and anything pertaining to the game. We had two highly competent officials, Scotty Boyle and Ron O'Leary. Both were quite experienced and had been in the game a long time. After our brief interpretation meeting, we shook hands and both officials made their way over to the Maryland side. It was at this time that our coaches, both Joe Ardolino and Jeff Clarke corralled me exclaiming "Coach, did you smell their breath? They had been doing some heavy drinking!!" Evidently, both had started to celebrate the holiday early in the day. I told the coaches, "You should be glad we're playing in the afternoon! If this were a night contest they probably wouldn't have shown up!" (What the reader must understand at this time is that there is a strong bond between lacrosse people and St. Patrick's day and by neglecting to celebrate this great day in some fashion or way, one could easily be condemned to the depths of hell for eternity!!) Believe me, Ron and Scotty were not going to hell!

It was a hard fought contest throughout. We came very close but just couldn't pull it off. After the contest I was approached by one of my coaches. He asked, "Coach, Are you going contact the lacrosse commissioner and file a complaint about the officials?" My response was "No, but I will contact him and request that all officials follow the same procedure and have a few drinks before each and every contest! That's the best officiating job I have ever had from Ron and Scotty!!"

HE'S GOING TO BE A GOOD ONE

SUBMITTED BY
CARL RUNK

Greg LaCour came to Towson in the early eighty's. He was good lacrosse player and we felt he had the ability to help our program. I remember his freshman year and how nervous he was about making a mistake and getting yelled at. We called for him to play the point position on the offensive fast break drill. He nervously took the position and to this day I really believe he was so emotional that he urinated in his shorts. Coach Ardolino said "Coach, I think he's going to be a good one. Let's watch him." As the fast break middie came down field his first responsibility was to throw the ball to the point man, who, in this scenario, was "Luke" as we always called him.

    He was standing properly, had the stick in the right position to catch the ball, and looked like a million dollars until the ball was passed to him. He literally did not move, stared straight ahead and was so emotional that the ball hit him square in the chest. He literally got shot by a lacrosse ball!! Not only did he get hit by the ball but he also got run over by the point defenseman going after the loose ball! As the players helped him to his feet he looked raunchy to say the least. Like an inner city statue that was attacked by 35 constipated pigeons!! Rough start for the "Lucas".

THE SPEECH IMPEDIMENT

SUBMITTED BY
CARL RUNK

Luke came to my office to tell me he needed a three credit course. I suggested he go up to the speech pathology department and ask the secretary to sign him up for my sign language class. Luke went up but didn't come back. I waited for some time and then called to find out if he had signed up for the course. The secretary told me everything was being taken care of, that they were, at that time, testing Luke in the lab for his speech impediment! I retorted, "I sent him up there to sign up for my sign language class. He doesn't have a speech impediment!! He's from Long Island!! They all talk that way up there!!

THE "VAN HEUSEN" SHIRT

SUBMITTED BY
CARL RUNK

I had an opportunity to speak at the National Lacrosse Coaches Convention a few years back and my intention was simple. Get the coaches to think <u>Towson lacrosse</u> when a youngster approaches them regarding school choices.

My plan was to dress up in a suit with the jacket buttoned all the time. (Usually coaches, when speaking, will have the jacket open or taken off) I spoke of how important it was to have your players and coaching staff believe in your philosophy and how you wanted the program to run. Everyone should be working toward the same goals. Be a salesman on and off the field! I then gave a personal example of what I was talking about in an episode that happened to me. "A few years back, I said, I needed a school colored tie for a recruiting trip. I went to a clothing store in Towson looking just for that. In the store, a salesman approached me and I told him I wanted a tie. He said 'we have ties, but we also have dress shirts on sale. I said I didn't need a shirt and that I only wanted a tie. He said the shirts were Van Heusen and they were 50% off! I said that really sounds great but not today. The persistent salesman then said "but this shirt has a 10 year guarantee on the collar and the cuffs!" At that time his delivery really attracted my attention. I exclaimed to the salesman, "you're telling me you have Van Heusen shirts on sale with 50% off and that shirt also has a ten year guarantee on the collar and cuffs!!?" His response was yes. I told him I just couldn't turn that kind of offer down and I wanted that shirt…with a tie to match.

I then proceeded to tell the coaches at the convention "Gentlemen, I went into that store with one intention….to buy a tie. This salesman convinced me I needed to buy a shirt along with the tie and I bought it! In fact, I am wearing the shirt right now, <u>and I still have two years to go on the collar and cuffs!!</u> "And that's the kind of perseverance YOU need in coaching! Believe strongly in yourself and make the players believe in your philosophy and what you are trying to teach!!"

I then got into my topic a little further and after a while I unbuttoned my suit coat. Shortly after that, I started to take the suit coat off. Once the coat was off, the hall exploded with laughter and applause. The crowd went berserk! I was standing in front of the entire convention with a shirt that was <u>simply in shreds and ripped to pieces!</u> I quickly shouted, "Screw the shirt….. look at what good condition the cuffs and collar are in!!! And I still have two years to go on the guarantee!!!"

There are times, to this day, that I meet with old time coaches and end up talking about, not lacrosse strategies, but if I still have that shirt with the guarantee on the cuffs and collar!!!

THE COLONEL AND BUCK

SUBMITTED BY
CARL RUNK

A few years back, late '70's, I was able to go on sabbatical while at Towson.

Since my son, Curtis, has a hearing impairment, my choice was to do graduate work at Gallaudet College in Washington D.C.. I wanted to learn as much about deafness as possible.

I was very fortunate to have taken a course from a brilliant young man, Dr. King Jordan. It was the most informative class I believe I have ever taken.

King later became the President of the same institution. Through our relationship we had become good friends. He was an advocate of running and would run in any available marathon. Dr. Jordan contacted me about his competing in the Maryland Marathon which began and ended a few blocks from my house. I invited him and some of his friends, two, who were also running, to my home after the race. I wanted them to stop over for home-made stew and refreshments. They agreed but stated they would have to be getting back and couldn't stay long. To eliminate any disorder, I had put my black lab,

"Buck", in the back yard while we ate at the dining room table. One of the visiting gentlemen was a colonial in the military and was wearing his light tan uniform. Buck was barking out back and wanted to come in. Anytime there was food being served the dog felt he deserved to be involved. King said to let him in, there would be no problem with that. I reluctantly opened the door and that dog sprinted toward the colonel, locked onto his leg and started to hump the hell out of it! I was totally embarrassed and grabbed the dog, trying to pull him off. The dog refused to let go and continued to make the ugly vocal sounds that dogs make when in heat. I was able to get the top of the dog off the colonel but the bottom part didn't miss a stroke! I finally got him loose and threw him back into the yard. I apologized to the colonel who responded not to worry about it. "Dogs will be dogs!" A short while later, my son Curtis came into the house and was really happy to see Dr. Jordan. He asked King if he had seen his dog, Buck, stating he would bring him in the house to show everyone the tricks the dog could do. As Curtis went to the kitchen door I shouted at him not to let the dog back in the house, but to no avail. Curtis opened the door and the dog broke through the room towards the colonel's leg like a heat-seeking missile! Here we go again!! Same sounds, same movements, same leg!! We were finally able to pry Buck loose from the colonels' leg and get him back in the yard. It was truthfully a very embarrassing time. Dr. Jordan and his running friends really got a big kick out of it, though. I surely didn't!!

After they boarded the car to leave, they backed out of our driveway and turned onto the street with the passenger side of the car facing our house. Curtis and I stood in the doorway to see them off. Before the car started up the street, the passenger side front window came down. The colonel poked his head out and yelled to us, "Tell Buck I'll write!!! The window went up and our friends drove off. I guess "Buck" made a hell-of-a first impression on the Colonel! When I think about that situation

and how embarrassing it was at the time, I get a big kick out of it now. Our dog Buck passed on a few years later...
...I guess he suffered from depression. Unfortunately, the colonel never did call or write!!

CHIC

SUBMITTED BY
CARL RUNK

Henry Ciccarone, an all American midfielder, played lacrosse at Johns Hopkins University under the tutelage of the legendary coach Bobby Scott. He later assisted Bobby with the team and eventually, when Bobby retired, he was appointed to the head coach position. Henry was very successful as the coach and won numerous National Championships. I have always been sensitive to the fact that as successful as Chic" was in this game, he was never selected as "Coach of the Year" by his peers, though he truly deserved it. That award, somehow, escaped his embrace.

    Chic was one of my favorite people. We shared many laughs together. I remember his being neglected in his final year of coaching after he had, again, won the national championship and I thought I might have some fun with him. I sent him an autographed picture of myself and told him if he were ever on a downer, depressed in some way, just to take the picture from its storage place and after a few seconds of staring at my photo, his depression would definitely be eliminated and he would smile all day! Along with picture, I sent him a statue with the inscription, "Chic,

You'll always be my "Coach of the Year!!" The statue was half of a horse ….. and, obviously, you know what half it was that I sent him! Chic was one beautiful person!

THE BEER SALESMAN

SUBMITTED BY
CARL RUNK

Chic had an opportunity to go into business as an administrator with his teammate and lifetime friend, Dennis Townsend. It was a beer/wine distributorship. Since he accomplished everything he wanted in the game of lacrosse, he was ready for change, I guess. He dropped out of coaching and started his new vocation. I was sorry to see him leave the coaching profession.

It was late spring and I was in the Syracuse area recruiting during the high school play-off season. My recruiting appointment was set for 8:00 am. I had some time before my visit and went to a local restaurant for breakfast. It was a big weekend for lacrosse as the NCAA Championship game was to be held in just a few days. I purchased a local newspaper and went right to the sports section. One complete page was dedicated to the big game between Syracuse and Johns Hopkins. The reporter was anxious to report the strengths and weaknesses of each club through the eyes and opinion of Henry Ciccarone. Keep in mind, Chic had been out coaching only one year. He was, obviously, slightly bias toward Hopkins and throughout the article, the entire page, talked about how Syracuse would break down, in most phases of the game, and not be able to match up properly against the Hopkins players. Believe me, Chic held nothing back.

I was surprised very little was done in promoting the Syracuse team in this article by the reporter since this was the home team. In a final statement, the reporter wrote: "When asked how he, Roy Simmons Jr., felt about Henry Ciccarone's comments Simmons responded "What the hell does he (Ciccarone) know about lacrosse. He's a beer salesman!!" A classic Roy Simmons response which brought me to my knees!

THE DOUBLE TALKER

SUBMITTED BY
CARL RUNK

Phil Burke, a well-known Baltimore character and double-talker, owned one of the most popular bars in the city. The bar wasn't anything overwhelming but it drew some of most important professional people in the area, including politicians, lawyers, businessmen, and doctors. If it was relaxation, a drink, and outrageous entertainment a person was looking for, it was available at Phil's bar. Phil was also a highly desired commodity at affairs across the nation. He would often fly to California in the morning to do a radio or television skit and be back at the tavern that night to talk about it.

We had just finished football two-a-days in the latter part of August and decided the players needed a mental and physical break. I called Phil and asked if he would come to visit our practice and "pep talk" the players. He gladly accepted saying it would be fun. At the end of our evening practice I called the players together. The entire team gathered in a kneeling position. At that time I introduced Phil Burke to the team as a former All-American end for Brown University. I told the players this was a good opportunity to have Mr. Burke explain the difference between football, as it was played in his era, compared to how it is played today. He would also touch on what it would take to be an All American at this time compared to when he played. Phil took off in his dialogue of double talk and was fantastic. The helmets started to come off and the players started to move closer in order to hear better. The kids didn't have a clue that Phil was really in his element. At the end of his talk, Phil asked for a quarterback and an offensive end to come forward for a demonstration on the proper technique used in catching a ball. He critiqued the two players, in double talk, as they tossed the ball back and forth. He said he wanted the quarterback to throw the ball to him so the players could see his style of catching. The quarterback was asked to throw the ball high above his head. As Phil reached high to catch the ball, his trousers dropped to the ground exposing his white skinny legs and him in his baggy old boxer shorts. Not an attractive sight. This was a thing he did when he would talk about the benefits of exercise. The players tried not to laugh but couldn't control themselves. As Phil pulled up his pants I properly introduced Phil to a standing ovation. The players fell in love with the guy and I probably helped increase the attendance at his bar after that ordeal.

BILL METZGER

SUBMITTED BY
CARL RUNK

My lifelong friend Bill Metzger, (Willie) is a well-known Baltimore character in his own right. It doesn't matter what bar, night club, or restaurant he would go to, someone knows him. Bill's sense of humor is his strength. He can find humor in any conversation and always enjoys a good story. Bill was a very close friend to football legend, John Unitas, and could be found traveling with John all over Baltimore. One night, Willy, (Bill), invited John and Rocky Thornton, at that time the manager of Unitas's "Golden Arm restaurant", to visit a small bar in a section of Baltimore called Highlandtown". This was at the time when John had his foot in a cast and was on crutches. The bar was a neighborhood bar that Willy's father frequented in the evening. The owner was bartending and drawing a draft when the three walked in. When the bartender saw who was with Willy, he literally froze while staring at Unitas and had draft beer pouring all over the bar! The three went to the back of the bar counter were Willie's father had a permanent seat. It was a super opportunity for neighborhood people to find out how down to earth and what a great person Unitas was. Everyone there had a great time. The next morning when Willie came down to breakfast with his mom and dad, he asked his mom to ask "pop" who he met last night. When she asked him who he met, he, in a very casual manner and non-assuming manner, said "Willie brought his friend Rocky and some other guy with his leg in a cast!!"

The top player in pro-football being introduced as "some other guy with his leg in a cast!!"

This evidently leads us to believe not everybody in Highlandtown was interested in football.

MOX

SUBMITTED BY
CARL RUNK

Willie's mom, sometimes referred to as "Mox" by her close friends, was such a beautiful person with tremendous love in her heart. It didn't take long to understand where Will got his sense of humor and his zest for life. It was from "Mox"! I loved to be in her company. She was fun to be around. Willy tells the story about coming home from work and his mom was sitting on the rowhouse front porch as she usually did. All the homes in that block had porches with a common ceiling/roof. You could literally step outside the second floor window and be on the porch roof. He asked his mom how her day went. She said there was a little excitement, not much. "Do you know that crazy Phil next door?" (Phil, next door, for some time had been receiving treatment from a local mental hospital.) "Well, he was up on the porch roof and tied a rope around his neck, forgot to tie the other end of the rope to the radiator inside the window and jumped out off the porch roof, hit the cement steps below and broke his leg. The ambulance came and they had to take him to the hospital. You know….the dumb son-of-a b_____ could've killed himself!!!!"

   "Mox" was one of my favorite people.

FRANKIE HAGAN

SUBMITTED BY
CARL RUNK

A few years back, I had to travel up to Villanova University to make a film exchange with my good friend Randy Marks, who was the coach at that time. Since it was an early morning trip, I asked my friend, Willie Metzger, to go with me. After making the exchange and on our way home, Willie suggested we stop at the small town, Havre de Grace, which is on the Susquehanna River, for lunch. He said "Havre de Grace was the hidden secret of Maryland, not to many people were familiar with it, and besides all the beautiful historical attractions, it had some great restaurants." He also stated that I've never been there and it would be a good experience for me. Little did he know that as a young boy I would accompany my grandmother, during the last months of summer, to work at the local tomato factory in Havre de Grace picking, packing, and canning tomatoes. It was something many immigrants did at the time to make ends meet. When I informed Willie that I was familiar with the town, worked at the packing house and had a number of friends there, he, in a contrary way, told me I was full of crap. I told him of my good friend, Frank

Hagan, a very popular local. I also mentioned everyone knew Frank and maybe we should look him up. "I know exactly where he lives!" Willie responded, "You've got to be out of your mind!!! That was over fifty years ago and, by now, he's long gone!!" Why would you be that naive to think he would still be here?!" Willie has a tendency to be critical as hell at times.

    It was decided we would forget about Frank and visit the duck museum which was located by the water. On entering the museum, Willie said he was going to make a trip to the men's room which was located downstairs. While he was downstairs, I met an older couple and asked if they could assist me. I told them about my discussion with Willie regarding Frankie Hagan and asked if we should meet while in the museum, would they approach me and say "Aren't you Frank Hagan's friend?" They thought it was a good idea and agreed to do it. When Willie came up from the restroom we walked around observing the various displays. After a short period of time, while coming around the aisle, would you believe we bumped into the older couple. They both stood perfectly still, staring at me while pointing a finger right at me. "I know you!" said the elder gentleman. "You're Frank Hagan's friend! Haven't seen you in years." It was at that time the gentleman's wife joined in. "Sure! I remember you also. You haven't changed that much. Are you going to visit Frank at his home? He just lives a couple of blocks away." Needless to say, Willie was totally stunned, didn't know what to say, and just stood there shaking his head in disbelief. And I was not going to let him know I was pulling his chain. To hell with him. He deserved the prank!

"TA-COOPA-COOPA"

SUBMITTED BY
CARL RUNK

It was during the ride home in the same afternoon that I told Willie about my childhood friend, Dave. I was a young boy about twelve and Dave was much, much older, about 14 and a half. Dave was really cool and somebody I was totally impressed with. We considered him to be a "Drape". A "drape" is a guy who has long hair combed in a "ducks ass" on the back of his head. He is always seen wearing tapered pants, like a "zoot suit." and walks with a cool swag. Some drapes were really cool, way out and extreme. My friend Dave was one of those way out guys! I thought I was cool but Dave told me I was a just a "square!"

I told Willie about a discussion I had at that time with Dave while visiting his home in Havre de Grace. I asked Dave "what are the cool sayings that the "drapes" are using nowadays?" Dave, at the time, was looking in the mirror, combing his hair, something drapes do all the time, with his legs stretched apart by about four feet. His gonads were not that far from the floor. He was really cool! Without even looking at me and continuing to comb his hair he responded, "Ta Coopa-Coopa". I quickly asked Dave what does "Ta Coopa-Coopa" mean. Without missing a stroke with his comb, keeping his eyes glued on the mirror, he said "If a chick walks by and you think she's wild, you say "Ta Coopa-Coopa!" "Or if something happens that really impresses you, you respond Ta-Coopa-Coopa." I vowed that afternoon I would never forget that word, ... "Ta-Coopa-Coopa!"

Willie, in an irritated manner, jumped all over me about the cool phrase. "Get the hell out of here. I've been in every bar, dance hall, and pot smoking area in Baltimore and I've never once heard that expression .... Ta-Coopa-Coopa!! Your friend was just feeding you a bunch of bull and you were just gullible enough to believe him!"

It was the same evening we were all getting together at a friends' house to watch Sugar Ray Leonard fight Alberto Durand on close-circuit television. While driving down to the home I told my friend, Leo, about my experience with Willie during the day and also told him the story about "Cool Dave"! I told Leo, that sometime during the fight, when it was really exciting, I wanted him to jump up out of his chair and shout out "Ta-Coopa-Coopa" as loud as he could. He agreed. When we got to the home we sat down on the sofa, Leo at one end, Willie in the middle, and me on the other end. It was sometime in the middle of the fight when Sugar Ray got the advantage of Durand and Leo jumped to his feet shouting "Ta-Coopa-Coopa ... Ta-Coopa-Coopa!!!" I don't think I will ever forget the expression on Willie's face! He was in total shock and bewildered. He just stared at Leo, and then he looked over to me as if to say "What the hell is going on?!! I can't believe this!!" I just looked at him and said "Willie, you're not as cool as you think!!" To really add salt to the wound, one of the other guys jumped up and shouted "Ta-Coopa-Coopa!" and started to smack high fives with Leo. What I didn't know is that Leo told the guy watching the fight to support him with the same call when he jumped up. It worked out better than my "ta-coopa-coopa"

original plan. Willie just sat there, shaking his head in disbelief!!
   Final Score = Runk 2
              Willie 0

THE HAMBURGER SQUAD

SUBMITTED BY
CARL RUNK

As a young boy, while playing 12-14 football, I would lay on the sideline and watch the local high school team practice. It wasn't long that I would be a member of the squad. I remember talking to my friend Willy about if he was going out for the team. He said he wasn't interested. "Too much work!" was his response. "I'm going out for the band. You can still get girls if you go out for the band!" I was thrilled to be a part of the football team and played on the junior varsity.

It was the end of our season and a select few were invited to continue on the varsity level. I was overwhelmed that I was one of the chosen few. Mid way through practice our coach, Irv Biasi, called for the "hamburger squad" to run the oppositions plays against the first defense. I had never heard the term hamburger squad before and wondered what it meant. The assistant coach gathered us in a huddle, and showed us the play we should run. A terrifying thought immediately crossed my mind, "Holy hell…I gotta block Big John Pepka!! John was a high school All American and an extremely rugged player who took the game seriously!!

When I was in the huddle I weighed about 140 lbs. By the time I got to the line of scrimmage I think I messed my pants and weighed 135lbs!! I took my stance and looked across the line of scrimmage. There he was! Looking as mean as a recently castrated brahma bull with snot and saliva running down his face. I dreaded what was about to happen. On the snap of the ball, Pepka came across the line, like a Mack truck, and knocked the hell out of me. I remember laying on the ground looking out the side of the helmet and all I could see was Willie throwing his marching cape across his shoulders, marching with the band on the adjacent field while playing the school song. As I gathered my senses and got up I heard coach Biasi ranting, raving, and screaming " It wasn't good enough…..run the damn thing again!!!" What a long, tough day. At the next days practice when coach called out for the hamburger squad, I determinedly tried to be inconspicuous and got in the back of the group hoping someone else might step up. No chance!! "Runk! Get your ass out here!!" Oh hell, here we go again!! After that practice I knew exactly what was meant by hamburger squad"! In college they dressed it up and referred to it as the "suicide squad". No matter the name … You still got the hell knocked out
    of you!!

WANT TO SHARE THE BILL

SUBMITTED BY
CARL RUNK

Years back the National Convention was held in Boston. It was always great to be with the coaches and just talk about contests played and different players. After the last session ended, a group of the coaches went out for a late dinner. On returning to the hotel it was decided we have a drink in an area referred to as the "book club" which was quite reserve and exquisite. Stories bounced around most of the evening, particularly about coaches not present. At the end of the evening the distinguished elderly waiter brought the check to the table. Dick Slasza, head coach at the Naval Academy, told the waiter he would take the bill. I was surprised to say the least. On my school travel budget it was going to be difficult to pay my own bill, and here was Slasza paying for the entire group! What a considerate thing to do. Maybe one day I'd be in a position to do the same thing. Dick asked that the bill be charged to his room. He then gave the wrong room number. I know because I was rooming with him. When he signed the receipt, instead of signing his name he signed the name of Al Pisano, the head coach of Army lacrosse!! He gave the waiter a generous gratuity and we left the book club. Slasza said he would like to see Pisano's facial expression when he gets the bill. I thought to myself he surely has a lot of nerve. I then retreated to my room to call it a night while Slasza visited another part of the hotel to socialize with other coaches. It must have been around 2: am when he came into the room ranting and raving. He was really livid. I awoke and asked him what the trouble was. He said he was going to look up Sam Goldmeer, a long island high school coach and "beat the hell out of him"!! I asked what did Sam do? "I'll tell you what he did!!! He drank all night and had the nerve to charge the bill to me!! He even signed my name!!!"

My good friend was really upset and I never did ask him if he met up with Sam at that time but I do know this! "What goes around, comes around!!" And there's no love between Army and Navy people!!

THE NAVY/ARMY GAME

SUBMITTED BY
CARL RUNK

One of the enjoyments of getting older is the benefits of having grandchildren. I can truthfully say my world now revolves around my grandkids. Each one, unique in his/her own way and also so full of love and enthusiasm. I am blessed with 11 grandchildren and am available, at any time, to talk about any/all of them. The story I will share with you involves my grandson Keith Alan, a ten year old at the time.

One of the most exciting chivalry's to witness is the Army-Navy football game. It is just so traditional and inspirational. It was early May when I called my good friend Major Carl Tumeluvich, Associate Athletic Director at the Naval Academy about the possibility of getting Army/Navy football tickets for the annual game. Carl explained to me that there were no tickets available and the game was sold out. I first thought he was talking about the lacrosse game but he quickly informed me the football game sells out early and quick. He said he would call Army and see if they had any available, but he doubted that. Carl was very persistent and finally got five tickets for me. I decided I would invite my two grandsons, Keith & Carl to this great event. Unfortunately, at the last minute Carl would not be able to attend so I then decided to take my next to oldest granddaughter, Shannon, mainly because she was available and in close proximity. Our Mottos operando was to get down to the M&T Bank stadium in Baltimore early, view the march on, and tailgate with the kids. En-route to the stadium I was overly anxious to tell the group how lucky we were, that I was able to call my friend, the associate athletic director at the academy and get tickets. And these were great seats! However, I had no idea where we would be seated in the stadium. My grandson asked to look at the tickets and responded, "Pop, these are really high seats, in the end zone, and far from the field!!" I assured him he was wrong, the tickets were great seats and we would enjoy them.

 As we entered the stadium we started to climb, ….and climb…and climb. We, then, went inside the stadium looking around. Keith Alan tugged at my coat and pointed to where we would be seated. He was right. We were in the last row up just a little below the lights in the end zone! While in our seats, as a naval helicopter passed by, I literally made eye contact with the pilot! The field was approximately 150 yards away, players seemed really small and the wind, at that height, was cold and unbearable. But we made it through!

 What a great game it was with overwhelming chivalry. Later, as we left the stadium and boarded our car, Keith Alan said "Pop, are we going to make this an annual tradition? I quickly exclaimed "Yes sir, we are!!" "Every time the game is played in Baltimore!" Keith Alan, in his young deep voice, responded "Pop…Do you think you could get tickets from another friend?!!"

 Kids sometimes make more sense than adults.

TIRE SIZE 30-45=15'S

SUBMITTED BY
CARL RUNK

It was the beginning of the football season and we were having a morning staff meeting in the classroom discussing the needs of the program and how we could make progress, staying within our budget. Practice was to begin shortly and we were finishing up on the agility schedule. Our staff was limited in numbers (4). This number included a newly appointed volunteer assistant, Frank Ryzlo. Frank was, in his day, a running back for West Texas State. He was overly enthusiastic about coaching and at times you would have to hold him back. Frank wanted to know if we had a "rope ladder" in our possession. I told him we didn't. He felt it was necessary for the agility segment and would really help in assessing player personnel. I suggested the use of tires in-lieu of a rope ladder and Frank agreed.

Al Kouneski, an outstanding football coach whom we were fortunate to have on our staff, suggested that Frank would be the person to search for the tires since it was his idea and he was the only coach on the staff to have a truck. Frank said he would take on the task of searching for the tires. He would have to find different tire replacement companies and select from the used tire piles. As we were leaving the meeting, out in the parking lot, Frank hurriedly entered his vehicle to begin his journey. Al Kouneski, who possessed an outstanding sense of humor, jokingly shouted out to Frank, "We'll need 22 tires, 11 for each side, and Frank, make sure you get size 30-45- 15's." Frank waved in approval and drove off. Later, Frank did not make the afternoon practice and we were worried that something may have happened to him. Midway through our evening practice, Frank came driving up to the field with his truck packed with 22 tires! The truck was stacked sky high with tires! I shouted out, "Frank, were the hell have you been? What took you so long?" He stepped out of the truck in his grey t-shirt full of sweat and responded, "Coach, do you know how hard it is to find twenty two tires size 30-45-15's?

BOB HOLCOMBS' CALL TO LEO

SUBMITTED BY
CARL RUNK

To this day, I still "hang out" with my crowd, a bunch of guys I've been with all my life. Some I met in the 1st grade and others I met through high school athletics.

Our group numbered, at one time, about 18 persons, but over the years that number has dwindled. One thing for sure, they were always available for a good practical joke! One episode that always brings a laugh to mind involves two of the guys, Bob Holcomb and Leo Wisniewski.

I played high school football, lacrosse and wrestled with both individuals and cannot tell you how close our relationship was. Leo had an old car worth about a thousand dollars. He was experiencing trouble with the car and took it to a mechanic for an estimate and possible repair. Bob, through telephone conversations with the other guys, heard about the car and decided to agitate a little bit. He got on the phone and called Leo regarding the repair estimate. "Mr. Wisniewski, we've checked on your vehicle and had to replace a few items, including the transmission and universal joints. The car is ready now and when you come down to the shop to get it, please bring a check for

$3000 dollars." Leo, probably one of the grouchiest individuals I have ever known, totally exploded, screaming as loud as he can, "bull-s___!! You were supposed to call me with the estimate!! Damn car's only worth $1000 dollars!!! Bob intervened saying "I don't care what you say, you owe me $3000 dollars and if you don't come down here with the check, we're confiscating your car! At that point, Bob hung up the phone. He then called all the guys to tell them about the episode, which got a few laughs.

After calling the guys, he got back on the phone with Leo, telling him it was only a joke, explaining that he called and not the mechanic.

A few hours later, the phone rang and Leo answered it. "Hi, Mr. Wisniewski, this is Stanley, from the auto shop. We've checked your vehicle over and found the cost for repair is going to be somewhat higher than the estimate we first gave you". It will be approximately $1500 ! Leo, thinking it was Bob again, went along with the caller saying "Don't worry about it. Money's no object! Do what you have to do and call me when it's done. I love that car and am not concerned about the cost!" He then hung up the phone and laughingly stated to his wife, "It's Bob again. "He thinks he got me!! After a few minutes, Leo couldn't wait to contact Bob to let him know he was totally aware Bob was trying to ride him again. Bob responded, "Leo, as the Lord is my judge, I didn't call you and I'm telling you the truth! The "old man," as we call him, almost had a heart attack, hung up the phone immediately trying to get in touch with the auto shop to tell them not to do anything to the car until he could get down there to see for himself.

Anything to save a buck!

THE LAST TEN OUT

SUBMITTED BY
JOE ARDOLINO TOWSON, '74

As we get older we have a tendency to change incidents as they truly happened. Exaggeration, over the years, becomes the truth, in order to make certain incidents more interesting. I'm not sure the following happened but some people will swear by it.

We were playing at North Carolina a few years back, at a time when they were the best in the game. They were a difficult team to play and were having their way throughout the contest. After the game had ended I was approached by an administrator from our school. He said it was a tough game and they were a good team. He then said he was standing in front of our locker room at half time and was glad he was out of the way when the players burst threw the door sprinting to the field. "Man, they were really fired up, Coach!!" I thought to myself, "we are ready to kick some ass!! Coach, just what did you say to get them so fired up?!! My response was, "Gentlemen, I am not too happy about your lackluster performance. I know they are a hell of a team, but I want you to know this, as the Lord is my judge, I will start the last ten players out that door!!"

Sometimes you can challenge their pride to get a good performance …… but
   not all the time!

MR. JOHN BLACK

SUBMITTED BY
CARL RUNK

I was fortunate to have been recruited by Jim LaRue, the head coach at the University of Arizona. I was at Kansas State at the time and not a happy camper and looking to transfer mid-semester. Coach LaRue told me in order to be eligible to participate in the fall, it was imperative I enroll in Phoenix Junior College in Phoenix, Arizona for the second semester. If I could pass 24 credits by the end of the summer I would be considered eligible to participate and also be placed on scholarship. The plan was to take 18 credits during the second semester and 6 credits in the summer. I agreed and was told once I arrived in Phoenix, I should contact John Black, a former football player, and a local business man.

It is important to understand this preceding bit of information before continuing with the story.

I was attending the 40th year anniversary of our football team. It was a beautiful time and exciting to see old friends. Arizona athletics has a breakfast function, the "Letterman Club Breakfast," which is open to lettermen of all sports. The breakfast is usually an outstanding and memorable

Along The Way

time. It gives everyone in attendance the opportunity to meet and greet old friends. As hard as it is to believe, there is quite a bit of drinking that takes place that early in the morning. I was mingling around the crowd after the breakfast ceremonies and came upon a group of old timers who were chatting away. I glimpsed at one of the individuals and to my surprise it was Mr. Black. All I could do was to stare at him with a smile on my face. He did so much for me and my family at the time I was in school. I hadn't seen this man in 40 years and here I was just a few feet away from him, just smiling. He glanced in my direction, looked at me, turned away and then quickly turned to look at me again. At that time I said, "Hi, Mr. Black, do you remember me? Carl Runk?" He turned and summoned his friends to come over. He wanted to tell them a story. "You know", he started, "40 years ago Jim LaRue called me to ask if I could assist him in supporting a player coming into town from back east. Coach explained the whole situation about what the player needed in order to be eligible." "This player and his newly acquired wife, who, by the way, was pregnant, arrived in my office in an old '49 ford which was packed to the ceiling with clothes and boxes. The tires on the car were bald, and there was a rope going through the back windows attached to another bald tire on the roof of the car!" "What a sight!!" They needed a place to stay, which I got them, both needed jobs, which I got them, and near the end of summer school I had to contact the president of the Phoenix College asking him to visit a difficult instructor to see if the player could possible do extra work to improve his grade which would enable him to register at Arizona. Not long afterwards, his wife gave birth to twin boys. While he was at two-a-day practices at the University, I had to drive his wife and the new born twins to Tucson. Until we found them housing, the first month they spent at Coach LaRue's home!" Mr. Black then pointed to me and stated ……. "And this son-of-a-b---ch wants to know if I remember Carl Runk!!!!" It was at that moment we all laughed and Mr. Black gave me the friendliest hug and kiss on the cheek a person could ever receive.

In life, some occurrences take place that will always be remembered. I will always remember and cherish my relationship with Mr. Black.

THE SOOTHSAYER

SUBMITTED BY
CARL RUNK

My son Carl was an outstanding lacrosse player and very difficult to keep in school. It wasn't that he was unable to do the work, it was just that he wasn't interested in that pursuit at the time. He said all he could concentrate on, while in class, was how he could develop and promote a business. We decided that he follow his goal, which he did in a highly successful manner. Sometime later, Carl invited my wife and myself to join him and his family for a Sunday day of relaxation at his home in Northern Virginia. At the time, I was in the middle of my lacrosse season and welcomed the opportunity be with my grandkids. During the course of the day we decided to visit the Occoquan yacht center, an entertainment area with a variety of stores & restaurants scenically developed on the Occoquan River.

As we walked along the walk-way I noticed a fortune teller's shop. Carl encouraged me to enter and ask the soothsayer if she could give me some insight on my upcoming game against Loyola College. I thought this was an intriguing idea and decided to see what kind of advice she could give me. Not to embarrass her, I told her I was a coach and had a tough game approaching this coming weekend. The lady looked me in the eye and while holding and rubbing my palm, she closed her eyes and shared her thoughts with me. "If you will work your players hard during the course of the week, you will be very successful". I thanked her for the prognostication and then went on my way. Believe it or not, that following Saturday we were very successful in that game and, to my way of thinking, I had an advantage, at this time, which could probably make me "coach of the year!!!" I knew the soothsayer!! I couldn't wait to visit my son and his family the following Sunday but, most of all, I was excited about meeting the fortune teller again. When we visited her place of establishment I told her the advice she gave me last week was right on the money. I mentioned I would be facing a tough Maryland team this week-end and would appreciate any advice she could give that would help us beat this team. After giving her the fee for her reading, she very calmly looked me in the eye, rubbed my palm and in a short moment looked at me again and responded "Don't press your Luck!!" We lost that game but what hurt just as bad was paying $10.00 to get that kind of a result. I never visited that woman again! I really believe Dick Edell, the coach of the Maryland team at the time, heard about this phenom, got down there earlier and talked to her before I did!!

So much for receiving the "Coach of the Year" award!!

COACH RON

SUBMITTED BY
CARL RUNK

Ron Marciniak, a dedicated football coach, is an individual very close to my heart. He is an absolute gem of a person who is highly righteous and compassionate to everyone around him. In his younger years, as a football player, Ron played at Kansas State and then played for a short time with the Washington Redskins. He later chose the path of coaching and became obsessed with this line of work. Most people will say their priorities in life are #1 God, #2 family, and #3 profession. I truthfully don't believe this was the case with Ron Marciniak. Football, and being successful within the game , was a major charge with Ron. He was the most "gung-ho" coach I have ever known, to the point you would try to avoid him as much as possible. This was very difficult to do, especially when he was your individual position coach. Ron would constantly test you regarding your knowledge of the recently given out scouting report. He would get your attention and immediately ask a question about the player you would be playing against.

"How tall is he???" "What does he weigh?" If you were wrong on any of the inquiries it was simply extra work for you after practice. "You didn't read the scouting report!!" He was a stickler on that kind of thing. And he could drive you up a wall!! As irritating as he could be, he was a good source of conversation for the players after practice. We all loved to talk about "what he did today!!" One example of a Marciniak-ism was being at home on a Sunday afternoon, watching a show on television and having Ron pull up in the driveway and come into the apartment. If you saw him coming, you instantly would turn off the TV, grab a book, sit in a chair and act like you were studying. Ron would ask you what you were studying, walk over to the TV, place his hand on the set and yell out that the set is still warm and that you haven't been studying but watching TV. End Result….More running tomorrow after practice!

PEARL HARBOR

SUBMITTED BY
CARL RUNK

Then there was the time Coach got us together and started to lecture on the upcoming game and the importance of knowing assignments, working hard and keeping a positive frame of mind. It was vital that we take nothing for granted. "Be prepared!! We will not get caught off guard!" he screamed. As he was walking out of the room he turned, held up his forefinger and shouted "Remember Pearl Harbor"!! I almost did a back flip! I recall seeing that same move in the "General Patton" movie! I was aware of his point but the example he gave was totally unexpected. Later, one of the players turned to me and said, and very seriously, "I didn't know they had Japanese players on their team!!"

"WATCH" WHAT YOU DO

SUBMITTED BY
CRAIG STARKEY, ARIZONA FOOTBALL '61

Coach Marciniak was a highly loyal and dedicated coach. His existence revolved around the game of football. He was completely obsessed with being successful and that involved the pride he had in the players he coached. He would try anything to motivate players to elevate their performance to the next level. An example of his pride in his work was an incident that happened one afternoon at practice. We were working on pass protection during the passing game segment. Our head coach, Coach LaRue, asked Ron if his offensive group was capable of giving total protection to our quarterback. Ron responded, "Coach, I'm so positive this group will protect the quarterback I'm going to place my wristwatch 4 yards deep on the ground!" "Any defenseman who reaches that spot can stomp the hell out of it!!" He then came over to the offensive line and told them "if anything happens to that watch you guys will run sprints till the cows come home. He was given the watch when he participated in the

East-West All-Star College Football game years before. It meant a great deal to him. This type of incentive to the defensive unit was overwhelming and they were completely determined to stomp on that watch! On the snap of the ball the defensive unit crashed through the offensive line like they didn't exist!! To an outsider it looked like they were huddled together doing the "Irish Jig!" They were screaming, chanting, jumping and yelling as loud as they could! The other coaches turned away from that scene and laughed like hell! Marciniak just stared at the remains of his watch. It looked like it went through a meat grinder. Holding true to his word, we ran sprints for a long, long, long time. Thank goodness Coach LaRue came out later to save us. And Ron, … he never attempted to make that kind of wager again! Anyway, who would want a watch that couldn't hold the weight of 5 defensive lineman!

THE ULTIMATE SACRIFICE

SUBMITTED BY
CARL RUNK

When I think of Marciniak-isms, the one that stands out in my mind is the time he got all the married football players together (13), yours truly included, and started to talk about the seasons expectations, individual and team goals and how important it was that we approach this season in the proper frame of mind. He said this would be a great season and how our head coach, Jim LaRue, was really looking forward to an outstanding year. "We can't let Coach LaRue down!!" He continued to talk about the role sacrifice would have on the team and how important it was. "Fellas', my reason for bringing you married players together is the following". "As you know, research has proven that having sex the night before a contest will weaken you physically and affect your performance in the game!" I'm asking you guys to refrain from having sex." We all thought he was just talking about the night before or before the game. Little did we know he wanted us to refrain from the engagement throughout the entire season!! It's important to understand, at this time, that this group of young men, ages 20 through 24, had tremendously high testosterone levels which could, at times, be seen running from their ears, not to mention the wives and the estrogen level <u>they</u> possessed! This was much more than just sacrifice!! He was asking for the impossible!. A short while after coach Marciniak left, we talked about his request and were almost unanimous in our decision <u>not</u> to follow his wishes……but we never told him!! The one player, however, a highly gullible individual, who would "sacrifice" and accept the request during the entire season, unknowingly had many teammates and friends, who did not make the travel team, visit his home during away games. Always nice to have someone visit your wife while your away just to make sure everything is alright!! I've often wondered if coach would have been willing to make the same sacrifice through the season as he was asking us. Knowing him, probably so!

TOWSON SCHOOL SONG

SUBMITTED BY
CARL RUNK

1974 was a fantastic year for athletics at Towson University. The lacrosse team had a tremendous season culminating with the NCAA National Championship.

The football team was highly successful having an undefeated season, only to lose in the Division III NCAA national championship contest. Our football coach, Phil Albert, a highly energetic individual with overwhelming charisma, tells the story about attending the national collegiate football associations awards dinner. At the banquet, when the master of ceremonies introduced the guest speaker, Lou Holtz, the orchestra accommodated by playing the school song of the speaker. Afterwards, there was the special awards ceremonies, including "Coach of the Year" selections for Division I, II, and III. Each school, represented by the head coach, was called to the podium to receive their particular award, give a short speech, and return to their table. As customary, during the intro of each school and at the end of the presentation, the orchestra would play that person's school song. One by one, each coach was supported by the school song. The atmosphere was ecstatic with excitement, applause, and enthusiasm. It was time to introduce the "coach of the year" for Division III. The announcer at the podium then said "The award this year goes to Phil Albert, coach of the Towson University Tigers"!!

At that point, Phil started to make his way forward but he was on his own. There was no support from the orchestra as Towson did not have a fight song at that time. Phil exclaimed it was the quietest and longest moment he has ever gone through ….. and even a little embarrassing. He felt like he was at a funeral!! After his short acceptance speech he started to return to his seat, again to complete silence!! I asked Phil what he did. His response was….."Coach, I just hummed the Arizona fight song, "Bear Down, Arizona" all the way back to my seat." Phil also said that type of situation "would never happen to me again!!"

Shortly after the convention and back at school, Phil sat down and simply by changing the school name and colors, converted the University of Arizona's fight song to the new "Towson Tigers" fight song. He was ready now for any situation!! "Bring it on, buddy, bring it on!!"

THE COKE MACHINE

SUBMITTED BY
CARL RUNK

It was at the end of the lacrosse season and our team was playing an away game at Vermont University. Because it was the final game day of the season, the result of the contest was highly important. Our score was to be called in immediately following the game. The NCAA Lacrosse Tournament Selection Committee would then compile records of all the teams and make the proper selection of teams eligible for NCAA Tournament play. We had some time, 30 minutes, before calling the university to find out if our team had qualified for the tournament and it was decided to stop at a local family restaurant outside of town to have dinner with the players before heading home. At that time I was responsible for paying the bill, which I did. I was given a large amount of bills in change, $1700 to be precise, by the manager of the restaurant and requested a paper bag to place the money into. This money would then be placed in a brief case which was on the bus. I rapped the bag up trying to seem inconspicuous, told the coaches I was going to go outside to make the call from a public phone. The phone was next to a coke machine. I placed the bag on top of the coke machine and made my call. When I found out the results, I was exuberant about our kids being selected. I couldn't wait to tell them. As we boarded the bus you could feel the overwhelming level of excitement in the air. It was so great to see the kids and coaches in that frame of mind! About a half hour down the road, Coach Clark requested the money bag in order to balance the trip bills. It was at that time, I got the sickest feeling in my stomach. In all of the excitement, I had left the bag containing the $1700 on top of the coke machine!! I yelled to the bus driver to turn around and go back to the restaurant. On the way back, I must have said the rosary a few times! As we approached the restaurant parking lot I looked directly to the coke machine. There were a few kids in front of the machine and the bag was still on top!!! I was out of the bus like a heat seeking missile, grabbing the bag and looking to see if the money was all there. The kids standing there couldn't get over what they had missed. "That could have been ours!!" What a great break. I often have felt I have a guardian angel looking out for me. The angel was surely there this time!

JOE SUGAI

SUBMITTED BY
CARL RUNK

As a young person, approximately 14 years of age, I spent a great deal of time with about 10 other youngsters ranging in age from 13 to 16. We would meet during the evenings at a little restaurant in east Baltimore. Our schedule of events ranged from flirting with the girls, talking about sports, to what was eaten for dinner. One of the fellows, Joe Sugai, an older member of our group, at 16, was quite interesting. "Shugs" or "Sugars", as he was known to the guys, was a good athlete, especially in baseball. We would often go over to the park and watch him play unlimited baseball for the "American legion" team. It was a solid league of amateur baseball. He quit high school in his senior year and took a position as a bell hop at the Lord Baltimore Hotel, in downtown Baltimore.

We all admired "Shugs" because of his adult life style. He had a full time job, didn't have to worry about school any longer, but most of all, he always had money in his pocket and could order anything he wanted from the restaurant. He wasn't restricted to a coke or splitting an order of french fries five ways!

We would seem mesmerized by his stories about episodes that would take place at the hotel during the course of a working day, especially the stories about the female guests! How many times I wished, when I was sixteen years old, that I could quit school and become a bell-hop at the Lord Baltimore Hotel!

One summer evening "Shugs" came down the corner and talked about what happened to him at the hotel during that day. He said it was a little embarrassing. The Detroit Tigers baseball team had come to town for their series with the Orioles. They would be staying at the Lord Baltimore. As they were checking in to the hotel, "Shugs" was called to the front desk to carry a few suit cases for some of the players. One of the players was Al Kaline, the all-time great Hall of Famer. Before going pro, Kaline, who attended Southern High School in South Baltimore, played in the same unlimited league as Joe. As fate would have it, Joe Sugars would have to carry Al Kaline's bags. On the elevator, Joe, trying to seem inconspicuous, kept looking down to the floor. Kaline stared at Joe for some time and finally exclaimed, "I thought I recognized you from somewhere and I know where it is now."

"Didn't you play baseball for the American Legion team as a catcher?" "Shugs" very humbly said "Yes"!! Kaline responded "Sure. "Hey fellas, wait till you here this story!" "We had a man on first base and a left handed batter at the plate!" The man on first was going to steal second. Pointing to "Shugs", Kaline said "you were the catcher, a right hander, trying to throw him out at second and in the process hit the left handed batter in the head with the ball, knocking him out!!!" The crowd on the elevator got a big laugh out of the story. Later, while coming down the elevator to the main floor, Joe thought "What a hell of a way to be remembered by someone! Especially a person like Al Kaline!!"

MY FAVORITE REFEREE STORY

SUBMITTED BY
TONY SEAMAN FORMER HOPKINS/TOWSON

I am coaching at the University of Pennsylvania, 1986 and playing Syracuse in the Dome. It's early fourth quarter and we are losing 19 to 3. As we face off the sideline official is standing in front of me on the wing line. My face off guy wins the draw but is trampled from behind by the Syracuse player and there is no call. I take the entire game frustrations of getting "killed" score wise, getting no calls in the Dome and now my face off guy is run over from behind so I let the closest official have it. As he turns to face me and throw his flag for my unsportsmanship manner and discourse I quickly ask him, "Do you know how bad an official you are?" He pauses with his action to throw the flag and looks at me considering my question, this gives me the opportunity to continue, and I state, "you are as bad as an official as I am a coach. Just look at the score!!!" He considers my statement, shakes his head sadly and simply puts his flag back in his belt and moves away, muttering as he goes by, "you are one sick coach."

LEE PINNEY'S FARM

SUBMITTED BY
PETER LAWRENCE HEAD COACH/ HARTFORD

One of the coolest things I have ever seen or been a part of is playing in the summer league up here in Ct and western Mass that plays at Lee Pinney's farm. Not sure what we call the league. Think it is the LL. Heard Lee is being inducted in the CT Lax HOF next month. The old timer still comes out and plays and he is well past 70. Remarkable man.

(editors note: I must say it really irritates me that this coach thinks that when a person reaches 70 he's an old man!!!)

The significance of his farm is it's like the lax field of dreams and I am sure anyone who has ever stepped foot on his property has great admiration and respect for what he has given back to the game. Plus many great games and post game events. He would feed everyone with burgers and dogs and fresh corn. A very special place. That is what comes to mind for me. I am sure guys who have been in these parts longer than me can tell you more about Lee and the farm.

THE SCHOLARSHIP CANDIDATE

SUBMITTED BY
ANDY COPELAN U. OF MARYLAND COACH

I'm at a recruiting event at UMBC and I'm sitting on the sidelines with a good buddy of mine, Kevin Warne, who now coaches up at Harvard. At the time, I'm an assistant coach at the University of Maryland. For anyone who knows Kevin, it's safe to say that he's a bit left of center. Anyways, it's the middle of the game and Kevin is getting antsy so he grabs a ball and starts writing on it. He hands me the ball when he's done and it reads "you are a scholarship candidate – Call me – Coach Copelan – University of Maryland." He rolls the ball to the end line and before you know it, the ball is in play. Sure enough, about two days later I get a message on my office phone from the young man who ended up with the ball. He was saying how it was always his dream to play at the University of Maryland and how he was thrilled about the possibility of our recruiting him. Poor soul…..

OLD BLOOD AND GUTS

SUBMITTED BY
DOM STARSIA UNIVERSITY OF VIRGINIA

In 1995, it was the Wednesday before our game in the NCAA semifinals with Syracuse. I had a little lump on the side of my face that my wife had been badgering me to have someone take a look at. I happened to be standing with the team doctor when she brought it up again and he arranged for me to run over and see the dermatologist at the hospital. I was in a bit of a hurry because we had practice coming up and the dermatologist said, "it appears benign but it has to come off, I can do it for you right now or, you can come back sometime". I told him, "you are good enough to see me, if you don't mind, I'm here, let's do it". He numbs it up a bit, completes the procedure, puts a small bandage on it and I run out the door to make practice. I figured I would mention it at some point to the team but it is early in practice and I am "yapping" at everyone trying to make a point about something. I am into it but the team is standing there, looking bewildered, mouths agape...finally, I ask, "what the heck is going on?" One of the players meekishly points to my face and I come to realize I have broken the stitches and there is blood running down my neck in to my shirt. I recall making some comment about the "blood and guts" required to be good enough!

DEFENSEMAN FOUND NOT GUILTY

SUBMITTED BY
DOM STARSIA UNIVERSITY OF VIRGINIA

In 1997, we were in the middle of a game with Harvard when a police officer came up to me on the sideline and asked if I knew where he could find Andy Henderson. I am sure that with a look of confusion and surprise I told him, "He's out there on the field, #29". Andy was one of our starting defenseman and earlier in the game with the ball in the opposite end of the field and everycne's attention pointed in that direction, he had gone over and whacked a spectator in the head with this stick. Seems that spectator had been riding our goalie unmercifully throughout the early part of the game and Andy had simply had enough. This person had gone to the hospital and called the police while being attended to. The policeman who came to the field allowed Andy to complete the game and then I accompanied them both to the police station when the game was over. Andy never really got into trouble because it was ruled that since the field had no fence nor rope, the spectators were intruding on the game. There was a fence around that field the next time we played at Harvard.

GAME PLAN ... "STOP THE GAITS!"

SUBMITTED BY
DOM STARSIA UNIVERSITY OF VIRGINIA

In 1990, Brown played at Syracuse in the NCAA, Quarterfinals; it was the final home game for the Gait brothers. Our plan was to slow down the pace of play early, make it a low scoring game and then try to make a run at Syracuse in the second half. Paul and Gary Gait were both on the wings for the opening face-off and each scored a goal in the first twelve seconds of the game....<u>Can that plan</u>!!! new strategy required! Syracuse went on to win 16-13.

THE OFFICIAL WITH NO SENSE OF HUMOR

SUBMITTED BY
ANDREW TOWERS DARTMOUTH HEAD COACH

Last year when we were playing Duke, the referee, Bruce Crawford got hit in the groin with an errant shot. He stumbled over to the sideline a few feet from where I was standing, and keeled over. After making sure that he was ok, I said "Bruce, it's a good thing that you only use that thing for pissing" only to have him reply with "F You, Andy!!"

BAD CALL AT DENISON

SUBMITTED BY
CURTIS GILBERT, NEW ENGLAND COLLEGE

The story I will share at this time involves my first official game as at Denison University. I was in my 5th year of coaching and had just joined a Head Coach who I had more experience than and he was entering his first year as a Head Coach at Denison, so we were both new to the program and flying by the seat of our pants. He gave me freedom to do and say whatever I wanted, as we had previously coached against one another in our previous positions, which was good because as a former defensemen and the defensive coach you can understand how we can all tend to get carried away and sometimes boil over.

Anyways, it was the first game of the season and we were playing against Kenyon college who was working on becoming an up and coming rival to Denison University, and were in the midst of their first ever program win over us. The previous defense had been decimated by graduation, and my new players consisting of freshmen and sophomores were having a very difficult time in grasping the intricacies of my defensive schemes.

It was somewhere in the fourth quarter and we were losing by 3 or 4 goals when we were clearing the ball and were called off-sides. The way we were clearing the ball is that the opposite field player could cross over only once the near side (and vice versa) player had jumped back on-sides which can cause some confusion if the referees are not situated properly. We had just cleared the ball with the far player, as the nearside player was jumping onsides, when the referee signaled off-sides and it would be Purple ball (Kenyon). That was all I needed and boiled over. As previously stated we were losing to a team that I felt we should not be losing to and immediately flipped my lid. I became irate and began screaming at the box side official "Don't give us a foul just because you aren't in shape to be in the right position. You cannot blame us, because you cannot see the game." The referee immediately grabbed a flag and launched it in the air and asked me to back away as I was now about 10 yards on the field.

I started to back away and yelled some more obscenities before completely losing it and taking my two pieces of "Orbitz" orange flavored gum and launched it at the referee and nailed him directly in the chest. He looked down at the gum slowly as it hit his chest and then fell to the turf and then slowly looked up at me. We connected eyes and I slowly turned and walked away like a dog that has done something wrong and knows it.

To my surprise the ref did not give me a second flag, but they did begin to huddle up as a group. My Head Coach flipped on me and banished me to the end of the bench where I took a knee, and found that he had also sent a volunteer assistant coach down to keep an eye on me and make sure that I did not do anything else stupid. I grew increasingly confused and curious as the referee's continued to talk, and when they broke the huddle, the ref reached down and grabbed the flag and to everyone's surprise picked it up and waived the flag off, stating that

I was indeed correct and the ball would be awarded to us. You can imagine how the other coach responded by losing his mind. Stating that "I have NEVER in my life seen a referee change a call, ESPECIALLY from an asst. coach. And how about the gum? Nothing for that?"

Well Kenyon did go on to beat us, and I apologized to my head coach and the team for my outburst and the next day in our film session we all reviewed the film only to find out that I clearly was <u>wrong</u> and the ref had made the correct call…..the first time!!

I also have a buddy who did not like the way the ref was calling a game of his in Texas and felt it was very lopsided. He called a timeout and told one of his players to 'Face guard' the referee for the remainder of the period. As told, after the timeout the player matched up on the referee and began to face guard him. They went up and down a couple of times before the referee finally approached the sideline where the coach was with the face guarding player in tow, and asked him "what is your player doing?" Coach Block responded "If you are going to keep calling the game for the other team, than I guess I have to guard you too." He was obviously flagged for this, and secured what I feel is the greatest move of all time…..

THE 25 LB. CONE

SUBMITTED BY
JIM BERKMANN COACH SALISBURY COLLEGE

We are playing Adelphi at their place, we both are defending champions and both number 1 in the current season. Score is tied 8-8 late in fourth quarter, great game and everyone is getting chances to win it.

We get a great stop on defense, quick clear and transition in typical Seagull style and get a 4 on 3 break, bang, bang three quick passes, down the backside and a one on one shot. You think the game is over, only a few seconds left and Adelphi's goalie makes a diving one on one save!! I turn around and kick the box cone on the sideline. Little did I know these where weighed cones and weighted about 25 lbs.(it was like kicking a ROCK) .

I turned to my assistant coach as the remaining time ticked away in regulation and said, "I think I just broke my TOE!!!!!" I could hardly walk. Thank god we scored in overtime to win the game and I could get ice on it at the tailgate.

From that point on (as a running joke), we made the rookie coach each season check the cones at the box before all games and make sure if they were kickable or not!

COCA COLA SIX PACK

SUBMITTED BY
CARL RUNK

Summer camps have always been an enjoyable way to make extra money while observing promising young athletes having the ability to play at the next level. I was very fortunate to co-direct a top level camp, the *Top Star Lacrosse Camp*, with Coach Hank Janczyk at Gettysburg College. It was in the early years, at a time when we were registering the players in the University Union. As many coaches are aware, when running a camp, individual payment should take place way ahead of the first day of camp! All monies should be deposited well ahead of time. Hank and I were very easy-going at the time and allowed some families to pay at the door. This meant we would have a substantial amount of cash on hand without a bank to go to since we usually registered the players on a Sunday. At this particular time, as the players registered, all cash was placed in a container…..an empty coca cola six pack box! As we were ending registration, I went over to the gym to secure the scrimmage vests for distribution. After a short period of time, Hank came over. I asked if the registration was complete and where did he put the container with the money.

Suddenly, Hank looked at me with a sick shocked expression on his face. Without muttering a word, he turned and started to SPRINT toward the Union. Now, in the past, I remember playing the Jerry Schmidt coached Hobart teams in the early years while Hank was playing. I can truthfully say I have never seen Hank run, as a player, as he did as a coach that Sunday afternoon! He had left the coca cola box, containing $8,000, on the front steps of the student union!!! While Uncle Leo was trying to revive me, Hank came back saying he had retrieved the box, and all the money was still there!! Totally unbelievable!! With people coming in and out of the Union, thank the Lord, no one bothered to pick up that container.

Lessons learned (2):

1. More pepsi drinking people go Gettysburg than coca cola drinkers.
2. <u>Always</u> check cardboard containers sitting on the side-walk.

THE SECRET HIDING PLACE (PART 1)

SUBMITTED BY
CARL RUNK

While arriving to the Top Star Camp at Gettysburg, Uncle Leo and I secured our Keys to our apartment in one of the better co-ed dormitories at school. It was an air-conditioned apartment and very plush. After getting adjusted I mentioned to Leo I had cash, $900, that I didn't want to carry around during the week and I was going to hide it somewhere in the apartment. Leo offered to hide it for me and I challenged him saying I would go outside the apartment while he found a place and on returning, I would find his hiding place. After he hide the money he beckoned me to return. I quickly went to the cupboard, above the sink, and found the money. I told him that's the first place a burglar would look, that he had no feel for that kind of thing. I then told him to go outside the apartment and I would hide the money. When he returned he literally tore the place apart looking for the money. He could not find my secret hiding place. I told him the money would remain there until we were ready to leave on the last day of camp.

Uncle Leo hard at work

UNCLE LEO'S ABDOMINAL PROBLEMS

SUBMITTED BY
CARL RUNK

We had an excellent camp with no injuries or parent problems. Our routine was consistent throughout the week except for one day. During the week we <u>always</u> entered the dormitory from the east side entrance but on this day we entered on the <u>west side entrance</u>. I wanted to see if I could get Leo to go into the wrong apartment, the one across the hall from ours, the one housing two extremely rough looking women. Not that there is anything wrong with that! On this particular day, right after lunch, Uncle Leo was prime. He just loaded himself with all kinds of food and was having trouble containing himself physically. We rushed to get back to the apartment dormitory. We entered the building from the west side, and with everything looking the same, it was easy to see how he may become confused. As we rushed down the hall I let him get ahead of me. He was ready to explode! He started to unbuckle his pants and stormed into the other apartment thinking it was ours. The screams that came from that room could be heard all over campus!! Can you imagine an old man, a stranger, with his pants half way down, running through your apartment, thinking it was his!!! I was in the hall on the floor laughing my ass off! As he stormed out of their room, with the girls still screaming, running across the hall, I vaguely remember him cursing me while in the travel mode. I know now why he was barred from all the gas station restrooms in Gettysburg!!

THE SECRET HIDING PLACE (PART 2)

On the last day of camp, with all the kids leaving, Leo and I packed up the truck with our equipment and were about to leave. As I finished tying the equipment down I looked over to Leo and said, "Hey old man, let's get going!! I'm going to take you to a great restaurant and you can order whatever you want!! At that very moment, it dawned on me that I didn't have my wallet with the $900 in it!!! It was in the secret hiding place. And for added stress, the non-american speaking cleaning people had already made their visit! I sprinted, like Hank Janczyk looking for the coke container, and when I got to the apartment, believe it or not, I forgot where I hid the money!!! I could not think of the spot and was totally frustrated & sick to my stomach! The supervisor of the cleaners came and we tried to locate the trash bags in the dumpsters ….. but which one?? I paid one non-english speaking worker $20 to look in the adjacent dumpsters (with Leo watching him)….. (like he was going to let me know if he found the money or not!!) It was one of the most filthy things I ever endured …Sanitary pads!!.....condums!!! Strictly sickening things you might find in a college dumpster, but to no avail. Then Leo, a very religious person, said he would pray to St. Anthony, the patron saint of lost things and go back up to the apartment for a final look. I thought to myself, "You gotta be kidding me!!" "Why would St Anthony waste his time on us!!" But would you believe within five minutes of being up there he came out waiving the wallet!! I stood motionless in the dumpster with my hands full of sticky trash. I wanted to hug him but he didn't want me to come near him! That little episode cost me $20 in the basket at church the following Sunday and a couple bars of soap!………. but it was well worth it!!

THAT'S NOT A KNEE PAD

SUBMITTED BY
KEVIN GATESFORMER COACH AT SHENANDOAH

I had the unenviable task of starting the first men's lacrosse team at Shenandoah University where I only had one player who had ever played lacrosse before. The very first day I went outside to start practice & I just stood there for a second. I was taking it all in watching the kids have a catch. I felt like Patton surveying his troops for the first time! My heart was jumping out of my chest with pride. After a brief moment, I blew my whistle & told my anxious young team of 16 men to, "Strap it on!" It was at that moment when I heard one of my young new players say, "It doesn't fit Coach." I replied, "What doesn't fit?" He said, "My knee pad, Coach."

I said, "That's not a knee pad, that's an arm pad!" He was trying to put one of the big strapping arm pads on his knee! It was at that moment that my sense of pride was overtaken by a serious fear of the unknown I was about to venture into! While the win column doesn't suggest a lot of success that year, I beg to differ. I will never forget that first year at Shenandoah or those 16 young men.

KNUTE ROCKNE?

SUBMITTED BY
KEVIN GATES FORMER COACH AT SHENANDOAH COLLEGE

I Learned a lot from starting a team from scratch. One of the things I learned is that I am not a very good pregame motivational speaker.

I played in college for Hank Janczyk at Salisbury. Next to my father, Coach Janczyk has probably had the most influential impact on my life, more than any other male role-model. He is a lot of the reason why I got into coaching over 20 years ago and why I still coach today! One of Coach Janczyk's best qualities as a coach, is the way he would get us fired up before games. He would get me ready to run through a wall for him! Well, when I finally became a head coach, I tried to be Coach Janczyk. I quickly realized that you have to stick to your strengths and be yourself. You can't try to be someone else. This was my last attempt at giving a pep talk!

During my fourth season at Shenandoah one of my roommates got cancer. He had also helped me out with the team a little bit, having been a pretty good player at

St. Mary's College himself. It was right in the middle of the season when I found out. I figured I would break the news to the kids before our next game & use it as motivation. I had these grand illusions about this great Knute Rockne type pep talk & them carrying me off the field & me bringing the game ball to my roommate after the game. Fat chance! Here's how it all went down. I am very passionate about what I do & the human element that comes with it. I tend to get very emotional about the whole thing. We were about to play an away game and we were in the locker room before the game & I told the team about my roommate. When I started telling them, I started getting emotional. I started crying & then they started crying. It was one big mess! Needless to say, the boys weren't too fired up for the game. They didn't even want to go out on the field! "We want to stay here inside the locker room with you, Coach!!" They didn't know whether to go play or give me a hug. We got beat pretty good that day. More importantly, the good news is my roommate's cancer went into remission and the last I heard, he›s doing fine! One of my players told me after the game, not to give anymore pep talks to the team. Lesson learned!

THE MILE AND A HALF RUN

SUBMITTED BY
RAY ROYSTAN HEAD COACH
HAMPTEN SIDNEY COLLEGE

The other day we ran our team's mile and ½ time at the high school track and, "along the way" one of our player had to stop to take a dump in the woods in the middle of the run. He utilized some leaves, jumped back on the track and still came in one minute faster than our slowest man. Funny but probably not book material!

You might want to ask Hank Janczyk about recruiting in Connecticut when during a house visit a yellow lab pulled a pair of undershorts out of Hank's travel bag (after three days on the road) and ran around the house with it. The mom was in a night gown and robe and chased the dog around the house, grabbed the shorts, and got pulled around the hard wood floor . . . picture that! Again check with Hank on that one!

FULL FIELD RIDE

SUBMITTED BY
JIM ARDIZONE TAPPAN ZEE HIGH SCHOOL

On a settled clear our goalie throws to the defenseman on the wing. The opposing team immediately jumps into a ten man ride. Their goalie was way out of the cage. At that time, I tell my defenseman to shoot it at the cage..... He turns and <u>shoots it at our own cage</u>? Amazingly accurate, I was just thankful he was below GLE. (goal line extended) I think only half the team knew he screwed up. Obviously a VERY teachable moment

DIVINE INTERVENTION?

SUBMITTED BY
CARL RUNK

I have always admired the strength and peace of mind that Hank Janczyk & his wife Cindy derived from their religious beliefs and would like to share a true experience that happened at our summer camp. We were into the middle session in the afternoon when a distraught young player approached Hank & I about losing a recently purchased stick. He said he had put it down, went to get water and when he returned the stick was missing. We told the youngster we would mention his loss to the entire camp during the various sessions of the week hoping maybe someone would return it, which at times is highly unlikely. It was later in the day when Cindy came out to visit. She asked how things were going and we mentioned the youngster losing the stick. We both believed it was stolen. Cindy very quickly said we should join hands and huddle together for prayer. As I was outnumbered I did just what she said. There we were in a huddle, holding hands, with our heads touching and Cindy saying a prayer about the players' loss. I can still remember glancing over to Uncle Leo who was scratching his head trying to figure out what the hell we were doing. Feeling a little uncomfortable, I was relieved when the prayer session ended. Leo told me later "you just didn't seem to fit in!!" Now, every year at camp, it had been our custom to have "give-aways" (donated lacrosse equipment) given to the players after the afternoon session the day before the last day of camp. The "Uncle Leo Give-a-ways" numbered somewhere between 25 and 30 items. It has always been a highlight of our camp. In order to win a given prize, numbered ping pong balls were selected from three separate boxes. The players were chosen by having their jersey number called out. On this particular "Uncle Leo Give-away affair, we were down to our last "give-away", a brand new lacrosse stick. The number was called and, as the Lord is my judge, the youngster who had his stick stolen came forward to receive his award!! <u>He had won the stick</u>!! What the hell are the chances of this happening! I just couldn't believe it!!! Later that evening Cindy came over to camp and I told her what had taken place. Her response was "Gods will be done!!"

Immediately, again, we huddled for prayer.

I must confess, after that incident, I would lean on Hank to ask Cindy if she could help us improve camp enrollment with a few prayer meetings during the lean years!!

FANCY PANTIES

SUBMITTED BY
CARL RUNK

In coaching we all have had the experience of having a coffee break with a equipment salesman. Sometimes that special time can be very learned and philosophical as was the time I relaxed with an old friend. For obvious reasons I'd like to refer to my old salesman friend as "Mel". As we shared stories about athletics, Mel asked me about another coaching associate. How was he doing? My response was that these were very hard times for him because his wife had up and left him. Mel wanted to know "did he see it coming? Didn't he pick up on obvious patterns?" Trying to act as if I understood what the patterns were, and that I was up to date on this type of behavior I said "I guess not!" Mel then said "you know….it happened to me and I wasn't even aware it was happening at the time until I spoke with a friend and he pointed out just what starts to take place." "First, dinner preparation seems to fall off. Then the wives start to go to the beauty salon to have the hair done. Next, they join a health spa and start to work out. It's an excuse to get them out of the house. The credit card expenses seem to increase at an alarming rate with the purchase of new clothes. The final key is when they start to buy new fancy underwear!! Now you know something's up!! "Aint no need for all that change in a normal family!!!" Mel then said, "Carl….that's exactly what happened to me!!" "I didn't even see it coming." "And I bet that's what happened to the coach."

    I was really in awe at what I had just learned and wanted to share this conversation with my wife, Joan, which I did at the dinner table. After telling her the story that Mel told me, I said "Isn't that something!! He didn't even see it coming!" Joan shook her head in disbelief, left the table and walked into the living room. After a short period of time she returned and she asked me "what do you think of these. I just bought them today!" In her hand she was holding a new pair of fancy panties!! I really got a big kick out of that. Joan's got such a great sense of humor!! (Or was she trying to tell me something?!!)

ANOTHER TIME

SUBMITTED BY
CARL RUNK

Joan and I were sitting at the breakfast table one morning just before I was ready to go into the office. I was reading the morning paper and came across a statement that I thought was really astonishing. I wanted to share this remarkable feat with Joan. I said, "it says here that Wilt Chamberlain, during his tenure as a basketball player, had sexual relationships with approximately a "thousand women!!" "Isn't that something!!!" "I can't believe that!!!" Joan, without an ounce of emotion, staring straight down at the table, while eating breakfast, quickly responded, "A thousand and one!!!"

THE LITTLE BALL COLLECTOR

SUBMITTED BY
CARL RUNK

Dave Urick, long time coach at Hobart College in his early years was very quick at scheduling scrimmage contests during a spring trip mainly because of the blistering cold in upstate New York. He would take his team as far south as he could on the funds he was allotted. We would usually play his team on their way back to the north. On this particular day of the scrimmage contest I noticed a young boy with a ball bag backing up the goals and chasing all the lacrosse balls everywhere on the field. Every time there was a shot out of bounds, we, the home team, would have to replace the lost ball with another.

Seeing this industrious youngster, about 7 years old, trying to make a living <u>collecting our lacrosse balls,</u> became a concern of mine. I summoned the youngster over and asked him what he was doing. He said he was collecting all the balls he could because "Coach Urick is giving me $5 dollars for all the balls I can get!!" Evidently Urick and his team had lost the ball allotment on their southern tour and were determined to find a way to recover lost balls. Since I didn't want to make a scene with that kid in front of all those people, the kid forced my hand. It cost me $10 dollars to get that youngster to sell me back that bag of balls, my lacrosse balls!, that he had collected and to have him leave the area immediately! Urick can sure be a piece of work!! One thing for sure, … I'm truly thankful that Dave's kids weren't short on lacrosse sticks that day!!

GOOD ATHLETES ARE HARD TO COME BY

SUBMITTED BY
DICK SLAZSA FORMER NAVY LACROSSE COACH

When I first came to Towson University it was way back in '66. I was a young aggressive coach trying to make a statement in the game of lacrosse. In order to do just that, I employed a very strict player conduct policy. Besides, teaching and coaching lacrosse, I was given the assignment as an assistant soccer coach. My philosophy on coaching was quite different from that of the head soccer coach, who was also the athletic director. We had played an away contest in another state and had lost the game. For some reason, I was somewhat despondent over the loss and felt all others should feel the same way. Evidently this was not the case. On the long ride home I sensed a peculiar odor in the bus and investigated immediately. After locating the source and individual(s), I was determined to bring this action of improper behavior to the attention of the head coach. It was determined that we would discuss this inappropriate action back at the office.

The following day I went in to visit the athletic director and discuss this matter. I remember mentioning that the youngster should be disciplined by being eliminated from the squad. To my surprise, the athletic director did not support my philosophy and had chosen to keep the youngster on the team. I was very livid over this decision. I told the coach that his decision would send a wrong message. I felt he wasn't supporting me or applying the standards we had given the players at the beginning of the season. I told him another decision would have to be made; the player goes or I resign. What is it going to be? The head coach, the athletic director, looked out the window in thought, in a very quiet manner, stared for a while and then said, (and I'll never forget it) "you know, he's a hell of an athlete and we very seldom get athletes like him at our school!"

Well, you know the end of that story.

<u>editors note</u>: In all honesty, Coach Slasza and the athletic directory never did see eye to eye on <u>any</u> situation in his first and only year at Towson.

COACH IS TRYING TO TELL US SOMETHING - DON'T LOSE!

SUBMITTED BY
RICH DONOVAN HOFSTRA– MANY YEARS AGO.

After winning three LI Championships (1971-72-73) at EMHS under Jack Kaley and Alan Lowe, we lost our opening game my senior year vs. Massapequa (future college All Americans - Mike O'Neill (JHU) Craig Jaeger & Tom Marino (Cornell). Upon returning to school after the game the sun was down; coaches had the seniors move our cars adjacent to the parking lot so they could have us run sprints under the glare of the headlights!

In snowy conditions (4 inches fell during a scrimmage vs. Elmont (Jack Salerno & Walt Sofsian) we switched to orange balls and played for an additional two hours. Practice included 5 "cross country" runs (3/4 mile); haircuts and curfew were strictly enforced.

At UMass, (1975-78) our annual spring trip was to Long Island so we could play at Hofstra, (one of the original Astro Turf fields). Guys would come up with mysterious injuries so they could sit in the whirlpool and thaw out! Home games at Garber Field; adjacent to Southwest residential area housing 7,00 students; there was NO seating; students walking to the main campus to attend class would stop, watch, drink and party. (Professors who had Wednesday afternoon classes knew the deal) Opposing coaches would refuse to play until the officials moved the crowd back. Traditionally the first goal scored vs. Syracuse would result in hundreds of oranges thrown on the field. Coach Garber would have to get on the public address system to avoid penalties.

LONGEST SHOT

SUBMITTED BY
BUCKY BRANDT (MMU COACH)

In 1999, Mount Mansfield Union High School's (Jericho, Vermont) goalie Joey Harrington scored from 78 yards out (from his own crease) against Union 32 High School (East Montpelier, VT) when the U32 goalie raised his scoop a little early and watched the slow roller go through his legs and into the net. The game was played in East Montpelier, Vermont.

WHAT ARE THE CHANCES!!!

SUBMITTED BY
CARL RUNK

My son Curtis had played football for the Maryland School for the Deaf. His biggest fans were his mom and me. We traveled all along the eastern seaboard watching and supporting every game Curtis played. I learned early in the season not to get overly involved in the strategy and emotion of the game. It was all "love labor lost!" The following incident heavily encouraged my accepting this policy.

We had traveled to the Kentucky School for the Deaf and, with other parents, were tailgating along with enjoying the early fall. Early in the game, Kentucky had the ball and came out with a wide receiver to the right. This player was, without a doubt, the best athlete on the field!! He was about 6'2" and weighed about 200 lbs. Strictly sculptured!! I was going out of my mind screaming to the coach that no one was out there covering him. "You gotta cover the wide receiver!!!!" But all this effort to no avail. I guess nobody could hear me! The Maryland Deaf school coaching staff did nothing to ADJUST TO THE WIDE RECIEVER! I JUST COULDN'T BELIEVE IT. There he stood...all by himself like he fell out of a plane, and we did no adjusting. Now the irony to this situation is that the Kentucky team refused to throw to him!! This was either a poor coaching scenario or a first class show of player discrimination!

The final straw that convinced me not to get involved in the game strategy was in the last quarter of the game. We had the ball on <u>our own 7 yard line with a 4th & 22 situation.</u> Our team came out of the huddle and lined up in a "full house T" formation. I turned to my wife and said "he doesn't know it's the 4th down!! He should be in a punting formation!" I yelled out, only loud enough to be heard throughout Southern Kentucky,

"COACH….IT'S FOURTH DOWN!!…….YOU GOTTA PUNT!!!"

An elderly gentleman, sitting in front and to the side of me, looked up and exclaimed with a strong slow southern accent "Coach never punts on fourth down!!!!" I could not believe it!!! I turned to my wife and said "that's it!!! I'll never get worked up over this team again!! It just doesn't matter and it's not worth it! From now on, I'm going into the tail-gaiting mode!!"

And now the icing on the cake!: I thought the coach was going to run some sort of "razzle/dazzle" but to my surprise he ran a simple "dive" play right…….from his own 7 yard line!!/…...<u>and made the 22 yards he needed for a 1st down!!!!</u> What the hell are the chances of that happening?!!! A Las Vegas Bookie wouldn't have touched those odds!! So much for strategy!!

(And parent involvement!)

WHAT'S A "BROAD?"

SUBMITTED BY
CARL RUNK

Although I was busy teaching and coaching two major sports in my early years at Towson, I tried to make sure I had time to support the kids in their activities. The twins, Keith & Carl, at the time were involved with recreation league football which took place every Saturday morning. It was on this particular Saturday that I went to watch them play. Their team was having a difficult time, and as often is the case, the coach was totally upset. It was halftime and the coach had the kids sitting as a group under a nice shady tree. I never had the opportunity to meet their coach, but maybe that was a good thing. He sure was impressively dressed. This I will never forget! Let's start at the bottom. He was wearing a brand new pair of "Riddle Ripple-sole" coaching shoes. They were the top of the line coaching shoe!! I couldn't even buy "Ripple shoes for my coaches! He had on high white sox with blue trim at the top. His shorts were royal blue with white trim down the sides and around each leg. He had on a white coaching shirt with the collar up and covered the shirt with a royal blue wind breaker. The wind-breaker sleeves were pulled up to his elbows. Above his "no-eyes" sunglasses he wore a brand new royal blue coaching hat. This guy was dressed to kill!! In his hand he held a clip-board, why, I have no idea! As he gathered his troops together he marched back and forth in front of them in a very upset manner. Then he stopped and spoke to the seven and eight year olds on the team. "Do you guys know what it takes to play football?!!" "Are you willing to make that sacrifice to be a football player?!!" "I'm not sure you are!!" "Do you think their tough?!!" At that point a youngster, who had only been on this earth for approximately seven and a half years yelled out. "<u>Coach…..their enough tough</u>!! I almost fell over!! Then the <u>best dressed coach of the year</u> responded in an angry manner "you guys make me sick!! You're not interested in football. All you're interested in is "BROADS!!" I have no idea where that statement came from! I almost fell over again! It was at this time a youngster raised his hand to speak. The coach shouted out "What do you want?" The youngster responded "Coach……What's a BROAD???" The other kids on the team, knowing the answer, highly excited and ready to answer, innocently raised their hands for permission to speak. They knew the answer! At that time one of the excited youngsters couldn't wait and shouted "Coach, I know what it is coach!! It's a girl!!! YEAH!!!"

    Over the years I have always enjoyed relating that story to my friends. Kids do say the darndest things!!

    P.S. (I forgot to mention the coach's white wrist bands with royal blue stripes!!!)

BACK UP THE GOALS

SUBMITTED BY
TED GARBER FORMER UNH LACROSSE COACH

During my first year coaching at UNH back in the late 70's (Lacrosse at the youth level was non-existent then in NH but a few kids played) a group of 12 year olds came to my office a few hours before our game and asked if they could be ball boys. I told them it would be great if they could back up the goals, ("back up the goals" means to return all lacrosse balls shot out of bounds) they were excited to do so. So, when we go out on the field for pre-game there are no goals anywhere to be found. The boys had "backed the goals up" 50 yards from the field!!!

THE NEED FOR A NEW BUS DRIVER

SUBMITTED BY
TED GARBER FORMER UNH LACROSSE COACH

A funnier one, but x rated is when I was coaching at UNH and we were playing at Maryland and our team was down there training for a few days before the game (Dick Edell always treated us well with fields and meals before killing us), however it was a Sunday morning and I was going out for a jog to think about practice and when I was in the lobby the hotel manager asked to see me in her office. I am thinking, "Oh boy, what did our players do?" (it was St. Patrick's day the night before). She closed the door and asked me how well I knew our bus driver. She told me that she had to send security up to his room because people driving in cars by the hotel were stopping and coming in to report that there was a guy masterbating out the window at the cars!!! I did not tell our players, but I told my coaching staff and sports info guy, and we all decided not to shake with the guy the rest of trip (true story). Check Sticks,

WHERE'S THE COACH OF THE YEAR

SUBMITTED BY
CARL RUNK

Dick Garber, long time head coach of the University of Massachusetts, was very successful at that program and a credit to the coaching profession. He was inspiring and admired by his peers. We were at the NCAA Awards Banquet years ago in New Jersey. This is an end of the year celebration where players, coaches, officials, and anyone involved in college lacrosse are recognized. My wife Joan and I had the distinction to be seated with, among other coaches, Dick Garber and his wife Mary Jane. Midway through the awards segment, Dick said he was going to make a trip to the bathroom. It was during that period of time that the "Coach of the Year" award was announced. And, wouldn't you believe it ….. It was announced that Dick had won the award and he wasn't even present to receive it! A short period later he comes through the door and unknowingly sits down. He then looks over to me and ask "Did I miss anything?" I responded "Naw, Dick. Boring as usual. Nothing important happened." You were just announced as the "Coach of the Year!"

WHERE IS YOUR ALLEGIANCE

SUBMITTED BY
CARL RUNK

It was at the same affair a bit later, we were having coffee and chatting. Dick Garber's son, Ted, was the new coach at University of New Hampshire. As fate would have it, both the father and son would need to play against each other during the season. I mentioned how uncomfortable this must be for Mrs. Garber to watch that game. Where would she place her allegiance? She seemed to be a loser either way. I will never forget her response. She shook her head and, with a "no problem" facial expression, said "This one, pointing to Dick, is related to me by marriage only!" "That one, pointing to Ted, I went through labor with for two and a half hours and gave birth to!!!" He and I are blood related!! "There's no question as to where my allegiance is!"

What a beautiful answer from such a beautiful person.

TWO SPEAKERS ... ONE BANQUET

SUBMITTED BY
CARL RUNK

In my first season as both head football and head lacrosse at Towson University I was contacted by a catholic high school in Long Island, New York to speak at their awards banquet. This was a excellent opportunity to introduce myself and our program to a highly popular school. It was going to, hopefully, benefit our program giving us leverage in that area. Back then, '68, we didn't have access to a school car or a rental.

My mode of travel was to take the train to New York City and, once there, catch the Long Island Expressway, another train trip! Obviously, this took planning, along with timing. However, I was capable of doing this. The trip up was a long one to say the least. When I finally arrived to the school I met with the football coach and he explained the agenda. He also introduced me to Lee Corso, the new head football coach at Louisville University. The "Modus Operando" for the evening was for both of us to speak to the athletes, parents, and staff. Lee ask if he could speak first in order to be on schedule with the airport. This was no problem. What I didn't know was that Coach Corso was a hot item at that time. He was just featured on the cover of "Sports Illustrated" regarding a player on his team. As the story goes, this player came into Coach Corsos' office and told him he could make a beneficial contribution to the team. The player, a hippie, had hair down to his waist and ear-rings. Back then, this was a "no-no". Corso was unimpressed until the youngster came out to practice and whood-em. The youngster could really kick that football and was highly impressive! Coach said it was time to review his philosophy. Result? It was decided the "long hair" rule should not apply to an outstanding athlete. Coach Corso had his banquet speaking game together, was hilarious, and had the crowd in tears!! As I sat and listened, I thought to myself "How the hell am I going to follow this act with my mediocre saturday night "put em to sleep" special!" It was at that time I told the high school football coach to just introduce me as a visiting coach from Towson University. "Do not introduce me as "our next speaker!" There's no way I will follow that!! "If you do……two things will happen."

"First, I will beat the hell out of you!!!" "Second, when I finish….I'll do it again!!!" When I was introduced I stood and waved to the crowd……And thought of my long trip home and how lucky I was not to have to follow that guy!!

IF WE'RE GOING, WE'RE GOING DOWN SWINGING!

SUBMITTED BY
CARL RUNK

It was during the same year, as head football coach, I was called to a meeting by the President of the college. As this was a rare occasion at the time, I felt quite honored and important. No other coaches or even the athletic director were privy to such an honor! I was to report to his administrative staff room at a special time and date.

I remember discussing with my staff of <u>one</u>, Phil Albert, that this will be a great opportunity to share our thoughts on what would be needed to develop a strong and respectful program. I jotted down on a piece of paper some of the more important areas that would need attention first in order to achieve this success. On the day of the meeting I remember the president's secretary escorting me to the meeting room. As I entered the room I was informed where I would sit. This was not a round tabled atmosphere, as I had envisioned, with everyone contributing in a positive manner. It was more like a parole hearing, with me seated in the middle, on one side of a long oak table and the parole board on the other side. I was welcomed by the president who, in turn, introduced me to the council of deans (3), the vice president , and the admission director. It was at this time I started to lose my visions of grandeur and began to concentrate on "what the hell is going on?" I was asked by the president if it were true that I had been visiting high schools, and handing out admission applications and school information to possible prospects. I said this was true, that it was a "form of recruiting procedure and all the schools do it." I was quickly informed the admissions department had filed a complaint, that this was the responsibility of the admissions director, (skinny little whimp!) his department, and not my area. This action was a definite conflict of interest. He continued to say that I should do all my recruiting on campus and my responsibility was not to recruit at any of the local high schools. Towson was a small school, at that time approximately 4000 students, and the ratio of girls to boys was 5 to 1! Not too many guys to select from. And, you know, there were probably a few girls we could've used! After returning to the office I told Phil Albert what was said at the meeting. He responded, "Coach, what the hell are we going to do?!!!......How the hell are we going to build a program if they are going to restrict our progress??!!!" I told him we might want to start looking for new employment but in the meantime I wanted him to take a ride with me up to the admissions office the following day. Keep in mind, in those early years anyone standing in front of an office door at 4 pm when school closed could possibly get run over by employees heading home. The school would literally close down. The next day, at approximately 4:30 pm, when we knew everyone had left school, we arrived outside the admissions department. Coach Albert wanted to know why I was leaving the motor of the car running. I told him I was going to get into the admissions office and get the box of applications that we would need for recruiting purposes, and I wanted him to stand in the hall way and start whistling if anyone was coming. "If we're going, we're going down swinging!" I said. His face quickly turned a cadaverous gray! I entered the admissions-empty office and selected the desired material we would need to finish out the recruiting season. I thought Albert was going to have a heart attack. With the large box full of admission applications in hand, we left the building, quickly got into the car, and headed back to the football office. With the new additional material we were able to continue our venture and proceed with the visiting of schools and athletes.

We later heard, from a reliable source, that the admissions director would be leaving at the end of the year, hopefully to take a job as a prison guard, and the president would be retiring. Couldn't have received more welcomed news. A fresh start is always well received!

REFRESHMENTS AT THE BALL GAME

SUBMITTED BY
CARL RUNK

A beautiful time during the lacrosse season has always been, for me, the middle of May. This was a time when, if you were lucky, you were in the play-offs and if you didn't make the playoffs you were out recruiting. One way or the other, a large number of the coaches were available to watch the high school play-off games. In the Maryland area these tournament games were played at the University of Maryland, Baltimore County. (UMBC).

A number of coaches would view the game in the stands while another group would watch the games from a hill alongside the stadium. The hill seemed highly appropriate because there was no problem with parents and it did fit our comfort zone. We were able to discuss players, coaches, or anything involving lacrosse without any feedback or intrusion. It was an enjoyable time.

Before going to the hill, I would always visit the press-box looking for a roster and making sure to come away with a sheet of paper with a UMBC letterhead. Just before the half, I would inquire who in our group wanted a hot dog and a coke. Once this task was completed I would write the following note on the letterhead paper: "Please give this youngster the following refreshments to be given to the press box attendants." I would then sign the name of the athletic director, Dick Watts. Once this document was prepared, I would then look for a youngster who might be interested in making a few dollars, tell him exactly what to do and send him on his way. To see the youngster struggling back to the hill, loaded down with the refreshments was a sight to behold! All the coaches got a big kick out of it and we ate and drank in the comfort of a low pressure environment. We were able to continue this tradition for about five years until we got caught. What are the chances of Dick Watts being in the refreshment area at half-time? Slim to none!! But he was there. He returned the youngster with the note reading it was going to be charged to my account at Towson. Some people just don't have a sense of humor! Can't take a joke!

I had completely forgotten about this episode until I bumped into Stan Ross, outstanding defender at Loyola College, head lacrosse coach at Butler and at this writing, the defensive coordinator at the United States Naval Academy. Recently, Stan, at a clinic, mentioned to me "Hey Coach, do you remember when I was a young boy, ten years old and backing up goals, and you would call me to take a note to the refreshment stand and pick up hot dogs and cokes for the coaches?" "I just wanted to let you know that before bringing the refreshments back to you, I would always make sure I ate one hot dog and had a little coke from each cup first!" We got a big laugh out of that. Great days! Beautiful memories!

HEY # 62 ... YOU SUCK!

SUBMITTED BY
MARK REUSS - TOWSON '78

I have always been blessed with energetic and loyal coaches. Mark Reuss, a player for me at Towson, and also a great assistant coach has always been there for me in times of need. He's like one of the family. I love him like a son. Mark sent in the following story.

"I was given the assignment to officiate a Junior College semi-final lacrosse game between Essex CC and Nassau CC." "I was really fired up about doing this contest and wanted to officiate to the best of my ability. A short time after the game began, I heard complaints from the stands. People were relentlessly on # 62. "62, you're terrible! Hey 62, you suck!!! "Do you know what you're doing?!!" As I ran up and down the field, this complaining continued on. They wouldn't let up! "I thought to myself why don't they give the kid a break. Get off of his back!! Running down the field I tried to locate # 62. Couldn't find him anywhere. At the next time out I approached the other referee. I said, "boy, they sure are on number 62, aint they? Have you seen him? I can't locate him. The other official looked at me and smiled. "Mark", he said, that's YOUR number!! And all these years I thought I was #64!!

DON''T GO OUT WITH LACROSSE PLAYERS

MIKE HEFFERNAN, LACROSSE PARENT

As you know my son, Sean, went to Loyola University, he didn't get married until he was 35. He married a girl who was in his same graduation year. I ask Stephanie (his wife), if she knew Sean when they in college. She said "I knew who he was, however they told us to stay away from lacrosse players."

In 1990 my oldest son, Michael, played in the national champion ship game against Syracuse with the famous Gait twin brothers. Loyola lost the game 21 to 9. After the game I left the game with Brian Kroneberger's father Greg. He looked at me and said you look depressed. I said I am, at which time Greg said it could have been worse. I said how possibly could it be any worse, and Greg said the Gaits could have been triplets!

Editors note: The Gait brothers were only the best Players in the game of lacrosse.

BILLY, THE NAVY MASCOT

SUBMITTED BY
TOM LEANOS, DREW UNIVERSITY

In around 1985, Drew lacrosse used to go on spring break in vans to Massanetta Springs, Virginia. It was an old retreat a little east of Harrisonburg, near the JMU campus. Dick Slasza was the head coach and I was the assistant. A group of elderly ladies would feed us family style meals and Slaz loved good food. There wasn't much to do in the area, so one night we find out that Navy (with David Robinson at center) is playing in the conference basketball championships against Richmond at the JMU field house. Dick and I decided that it would be a great idea to take the team to the game.

Being the former head coach at Navy for ten years prior to becoming the AD and head coach at Drew, Dick still had a navy cap which he would occasionally wear. When we went on Spring break, we would load the team into vans, and pull U-Haul trailers with all of our equipment and so forth behind the vans.

As we get into the parking lot the night of the game, there's a pretty big crowd and the campus security and local traffic officers direct us to park on the other side of the interstate because of the congestion around the arena. Not wanting to be late to the game, let alone have to walk too far to get to the arena, Dick puts on his Navy cap and drives back around to the preferred parking right by the arena. As the officers approach the van to direct us away from the area, Dick rolls down the window and with a poker face, tells the security guy that he is on official duty from the Naval Academy and he is hauling "Billy" the Navy goat mascot in the U-Haul and that we have to park right next to the arena to unload the mascot. The officer directed us to the overhead door right by the floor entrance.

    Dick didn't have to walk!

WRONG GOAL, SON!

SUBMITTED BY
DAN MULHOLLAND MT. ST. VINCENT COLLEGE

Way back when, in 1976 I started a high school team. In our 2nd game I realized I had a very good middie, blessed with speed. In a 2-2 tie, late in the 4th quarter I needed Josh to take the ball from behind the goal to run it up field for a clear. He had just been in and was winded. He got the ball and when the ref blew the whistle, Josh took off like a rocket, turned the cage and to the dismay of our goalie and team, scored on us. After the initial embarrassment ended, he put in the last 2 goals and a brand new team started out 2 and 0.

PENALTY IN THE SNOW

SUBMITTED BY
J.B. CLARKE, HEAD LACROSSE COACH LIMESTONE COLLEGE

In the mid-nineties I was the assistant to Mike Pressler at Duke. Mike had been the head coach at Ohio Wesleyan for years and had a great rivalry with Hobart. Hobart was now DI and we were in Geneva playing the Statesmen. Mike is as intense as any man and on this day he was in rare form. His team was ready to play, the weather was good for Geneva in April, and Walt Munzie was the Referee. You may remember Mike Curtis - the great linebacker for the Colts - his son, Clay, was on the Blue Devil team. Walt was a great official and knew Mike from his years at OWU. By the end of the first half, we are beating Hobart pretty good and went inside for halftime. When we came back outside 7 minutes later the weather had changed - as it only can in Geneva. Mike was certain that Hobart was going to come back now that there was snow covering the field. Walt and his crew were shuffling along the boundary lines trying to keep the field playable. Mike was back to his pre-game fevered pitch and the team reacted well keeping the lead and extending it more into the fourth quarter. It was time for Clay Curtis to go into the game and play. Clay was a big kid, fast, strong, put together like his All-Pro father. And, boy was he fast! The field is covered with snow by now and slippery as heck. Hobart makes a save and outlets the ball to the middie who is streaking up the field. Pressler grabs Clay and sends him onto the field as a D-Middie in transition to the defensive end. Only problem is that we have not gotten a middie off the field yet. Clay gets about fifteen yards on the field before Coach Pressler recognizes the situation (none of the frozen officials had noticed it either) and calls frantically for Clay to get off the field. As Clay is approaching the substitution box Coach Pressler moves quickly into the box to grab Clay. Because of the snow, sleet and grass field Clay cannot slow down. Just as Clay gets to the box he and Pressler are about to collide when Pressler (former All-American lacrosse and football player at W&L) raises his forearm instinctively to protect himself. Clay and Coach have an All-Pro collision! Clay goes down as Mike's forearm hits his chest and his feet fly out from under him right there in the middle of the substitution box. The next thing you hear is an official's whistle. The next thing you see is a flag flying into the substitution box and landing right in between Pressler and Curtis. Walt Munzie had looked over just in time to see Pressler and his player collide. He blew the whistle and threw the flag. When asked by Coach Pressler what the flag was for - in a way that only Walt Munzie could react - Walt said to Mike; "I honestly don't know Coach but you just can't do - THAT!" Mike Curtis, all pro football player for the Baltimore Colts, told us at the tailgate party following the win that it was the best hit he had seen in years.

CAN YOU GUESS WHAT I'M THINKING

SUBMITTED BY
LARS TIFFANY BROWN UNIVERSITY

An exchange between John Haus, former all-american and Washington College coach, and an official during Haus' Washington College tenure.

Washington College is having a rough go of it (I forget the opponent), and John Haus vents on one of the officials. "Can I get a penalty for what I am thinking?" he asks the official. The reply from the official was no. "Good" says Haus "because I think you're an a__hole." No penalty was called.

submitted by Lars Tiffany Brown University

HALF TIME BOXING MATCH

SUBMITTED BY
CARL RUNK

The National Junior College Lacrosse Championship game is usually played the second Sunday in May, which is also "Mothers Day". Being aware that this was a "must" game to see for recruiting purposes and also how important it was to maintain a pleasant and happy home life, I would usually take my wife, Joan, to the contest with me. I did this for a long number of years. Joan loved to watch lacrosse and enjoyed evaluating players, as to the best on the field. She would then ask for my evaluation, compare it with hers, and then demand to know why I selected certain players. The important thing is I was able to watch the game and be with her on this special day.

This particular year the game was to be played at Anne Arundel Community College in Anne Arundel, Maryland. As was our tendency, we arrived early, purchased a program, and found seats at the end of the bleachers, away from the crowd. The teams participating for the championship were Herkimer CC., coached by Paul Werham, and Nassau CC., coached by Richie Speckman. This was predicted to be a shoot-out of a game, with both teams showing a high scoring profile.

The first half was well played with Nassau ahead by a couple goals. At half time, because there were no dressing rooms available, each team took a section of opposing end-zones for the fifteen minute break. Speckman's team was at the North end of the field and Paul's team was at the south end, just below where Joan and I were seated. Great!! I would have an opportunity to hear a half time pep/strategy talk! I did not, however, take into consideration the fact that Paul was highly emotional and possessed an extremely strong New York accent.

With him stomping the ground, flaring his arms, and shouting out words and sentences that were impossible to interpret, I would have had more success understanding Kalid Akar Mujari giving a lecture in the men's room at the Pennsylvania Train Station! But, remarkably, the kids understood him. Near the end of the 15 minute break, two players stood up and started to fight. I remarked to Joan, "Oh my gosh" look, their fighting amongst themselves!" Then two other players stood up and started to fight...... Then the whole team got up and started to beat the hell out of each other. I remember telling Joan, "He's lost control of his team! This is embarrassing!" Paul just stood there watching ….. Then after a short period of time he looked at his watch and gave a loud double whistle. The kids stopped immediately, grabbed their sticks and huddled together for a "Herkimer" chant! They proceeded to walk over to the sidelines, like nothing had happened, preparing for the second half. Would you believe they played great the second half winning the NCAA title! It was one of the most extraordinary motivational techniques I have ever seen. I later questioned Paul about this method of motivating. His response was:

"What happened at half time of the game against Nassau was that the players were not playing hard enough so we decided to pair them up and have them do a little boxing with no hitting below the neck - this is something the guys did all the time on their own."

A different kind of strategy……..but it worked!!!

With my luck, if I tried something like this I would probably lose half my team with half-time injuries. But most importantly, my job!!

MY SON DESERVES A FULL RIDE

SUBMITTED BY
TOM GRAVANTE, COACH, MOUNT ST. MARY'S UNIVERSITY

I'm pretty certain many coaches have recruiting stories about overbearing parents and their evaluation on their son's ability to play the game. This story may help parents learn better recruiting etiquette towards coaches.

This particular father, whom many, if not all the MD-D-1 lacrosse coaches know, was notorious for his comments on the ability of his son and his worth both financially and athletically to my program.

After my encounter w/, let's call him: Mr. Conceded, in my office for more time than I would care to spend w/ someone like this. I finally managed not only to get him out of my office chair, but out of my office. Yes, he somehow bam-boozeled me and the next thing I knew, I was sitting on my office couch and he was using my computer to find an online playing video of his son.

None the less, I agreed to come watch his son play at a fall event. When I reach the High School, I called Mr. Conceded to find out what field his son was playing on and what # he was wearing?

His reply: "Coach Gravante come to field 2 and when you have found the best player, you will have found my son!" Not to dis-credit the young man as he was a solid player, I made an offer to the family. His father replied back and said: "Quite honestly Coach Gravante, and not to be disrespectful, but your offer is too low as I feel my son is worth a full ride! I replied, then you better call Coach Meade, the head coach at Navy!

Update as far as I know, he went to NAPS and would be on his way to Coach Meade that fall. Good luck Coach Meade, God bless, and way to jump on that grenade for the rest of us Maryland coaches!

YOUR MISSING A GREAT GAME

ANONYMOUS

Just a quick story about one of the great old school officials (now deceased) Joe Mars from the Upstate NY area.

Refereeing a game in the Empire 8 league one day - Joe was being hounded relentlessly by one of the more vocal head coaches in the area. The coach yelled out sarcastically midway through the 3rd period "Hey Joe, You're missing a great game"! To this he quipped "I know Coach - I got assigned to this one instead!" Head coach

SPORT PYSCHOLOGY

SUBMITTED BY
SID JAMIESON, BUCKNELL UNIVERSITY

We were playing away at one of our rival schools. If you have ever played at this school the playing field is located on top of a mountain and the weather conditions are worse than playing on the Naval Academy's artificial game field next to the water in early spring. The point I'm trying to make is it is a tremendously ice cold wind constantly blowing and it draws from the focus you'd want your players to have. They don't think about the importance of the game as much as they think about "When is this game ever going to end!!

It was a difficult game that we felt very confident about but just couldn't get our way because of a stubborn group of opposing players, a good goalie, and a bit of overconfidence. Being behind by a few goals at half-time I told the team to get on the bus. The players thought I was doing this to keep them warm but my strategy was to have them believe I had forfeited the game and we were headed home. I told the bus driver to start up the motor and head out.

"We're out of here!" The players started shouting, wanting to know what the heck we were doing. I told them they weren't interested in playing lacrosse and I was not going to sit through another half of their pathetic performance! The bus was in an uproar! "Stop the bus, coach. We'll show you we can do a hell of a lot better!" I told them if the play didn't improve I'm calling the game. Well, the kids played great the second half and we won the game. Thank goodness, because I don't know how I would explain my strategy to my A.D.

So much for sport psychology!!

ROAD TRIP TO REMEMBER

SUBMITTED BY
DAN C. WITMER OSWEGO COLLEGE

I'm pretty sure it was 1996; we were making a two and a half-hour trip up to Canton, NY to play at St. Lawrence University. It was an unusually sunny and warm day, and when we left the Oswego campus, the bus's rooftop vent was open (I don't recall if <u>we</u> opened the vent or if the bus driver had opened it, but who <u>opened</u> the vent wouldn't really matter).

As we made our way into the North Country, the skies started to turn gray, and it looked like it might start raining. Players sitting in the seats under the vent started to worry about their fate if it started to rain. The decision was made to close the vent while the bus was in motion (why bother the bus driver?).

Now, I'm not sure how the decision was made, if he volunteered or if was elected, but freshman Bryan Morelli, who stood about 5'7 and weighed about 135 lbs, was soon standing on two adjacent armrests, and teammates were lifting him so he could reach the vent – which folded forward on the bus's roof – so he could close it. With half his body sticking out, Bryan struggled to lean forward and pull the vent closed.

While the wind resistance probably made closing the vent difficult, once Bryan managed to finally get the vent lifted just a little bit, the vent lid sprung closed with such a force that it knocked Bryan out of the hole, and he collapsed into the aisle with bruises to his head and his arms (the vent lid hit him in the head; his arms were banged up as he fell back through the hole).

Not fully realizing the injuries he'd incurred, the entire busload of Lakers laughed at the sight of their teammate being thrown to the bus floor (keep in mind that all of this happened at speeds of about 60 mph barreling north on Rt 11). However, when Bryan managed to get to his feet and the damage was visible, we rushed the athletic trainer to his aid. Of course, as luck would have it, the medical kit was packed in the storage area below the bus, so we had to make a stop for first aid supplies.

Bryan got medical help, and we continued on our way. If I've got the year right, we won the game, and Bryan watched from the sidelines. The story of his misadventure has been told and re-told among Oswego players for years; now everyone knows the story.

Editor's note - It's the first time I've heard the story!!!

THE PENALTY NOT CALLED

SUBMITTED BY
CARL RUNK

Bobby Sandel, longtime player, coach, lacrosse official and very good friend, residing in the Charlottesville, Virginia area, was usually one of the officials teams would get if they were contesting the University of Virginia in lacrosse. He was highly qualified in officiating and in great demand in Virginia to do games.

It was a time in lacrosse when the growth and development of officiating was just evolving in that area. If Bobby wasn't involved in your contest you could be in for a long day!

We were playing Virginia at Charlottesville and the game wasn't going as we had hoped. It was one of those days when the ball didn't roll in our direction. We weren't a bad team but Virginia was just outstanding and loaded with talent. Every call seemed to be against us and it was becoming frustrating. As we all know, when things aren't going good in the game, coaches have a tendency to put the blame on someone or something other than themselves. It surely can't be the coach's inability to coach! No way!! We're above that! Most of the time, when a team is losing, it's usually the officiating. Our team was losing and we were not getting any calls. It didn't matter what happened……when the whistle would blow, it was against us. And Bobby was making all the calls.

Obviously, I wasn't a happy camper and tried numerous times to vent my frustrations, but to no avail. He didn't want to hear it! Late in the contest a situation arose where the ball was loose with one of our players trying to scoop it up. He was completely surrounded by Virginia players who quickly annihilated the poor soul! I thought "hey, we finally got one." To my surprise, Bobby didn't call a thing! I couldn't believe it and started on the field to express my opinion. Bobby came over and asked "Carl, what the hell is the problem?" I quickly responded by pointing to my player that was involved in the altercation. "Bobby, you should have given my player a penalty and you didn't!! That's the problem!!" He responded, "what the hell are you talking about?!!" I exclaimed "You missed the call, pal. My player should get a penalty for carrying a damn Virginia player around on his back!!" He looked at me, shook his head in disgust and said "Carl, get the hell off the field before I call a penalty on you!"

It's funny how we remember old friends!

A MEMORY OF ED PURCELL

ANONYMOUS COACH
OSWEGO COLLEGE

Ed Purcell was an All-American defenseman at RIT, recruited from Levittown by Coach Bill Tierney when he made the jump from HS coach to college coach. Ed was a big man, and on the field and off, he always made his presence known in an impressive manner.

Soon after finishing his playing days at RIT, Ed was hired as the head coach at Keuka College. It was a very young program, and the school had recently added a few men's sports to increase their male enrollment (the school had previously been an all-women's college).

Keuka's roster often had just 17 or 18 players, but under Ed's leadership and coaching, they battled hard for 60 minutes in every game. I remember wondering what it would be like to practice with less than 20 players, and I remember marveling at his players for their stamina, conditioning, and grit.

In 1992 we hosted Keuka in one of the worst examples of Central New York spring weather. The game started in decent conditions, but sometime in the first half the skies just opened up. The temperatures dropped, the rain poured down, and both teams were drenched to the bone. We had recently purchased a team set of warm-up jackets and pants, and while they weren't Gore-Tex, they helped our players a little.

However, no one on the Keuka sideline was as fortunate, including Coach Purcell. He was dressed in a pair of sweatpants and a T-shirt. Looking back now, I wish I had offered him another layer, although I'm not sure anything I could have offered would have fit him. The weather was so bad that at halftime, we went into our locker room and players stood in hot showers – fully dressed in their uniforms – just so they could warm up. Getting dry wasn't ever considered; getting warm was the concern. Players changed gloves and went out for the second half. Maybe the weather was a factor, but things went our way on the field that day. We had a huge lead and the weather just kept getting worse. At some point in the fourth quarter, referee Curt Lingenfelter came to me and suggested we run the clock to minimize the damage. We were ahead by a lot, my own players were frozen and soaked to the bone, so I agreed, assuming that Curt had also run the suggestion by Coach Purcell.

Well, as it turned out, he hadn't. Soon after we scored another goal, Ed noticed that the score clock hadn't stopped, and he let me know that our clock was cheating his kids out of game time. Assuming that he knew about our agreement, I reminded him that we had decided to run the clock for the rest of the game.

To put it mildly, Ed snapped. He screamed at Curt, and then he screamed at me. No matter how hard it was raining, no matter how cold he or his players, were, and no matter what the score was, he didn't like the idea of being left out, and when I realized the situation, I completely understood where he was coming from. Curt apologized and tried to explain himself, but Ed would have none of it. He battled for his players, and he was absolutely in the right.

Ed Purcell was a passionate, loyal, and otherwise very amiable man. That one incident, on that miserably cold and wet Oswego afternoon, personified his competitiveness and his integrity.

I miss him very much.

"I DON'T CARE - I DON'T CARE

SUBMITTED BY
NICK CARROLL - HIGH SCHOOL

This actually happened this year in a middle school game in San Diego. There was a face off violation and just as the whistle blew at midfield to start play with the offended team in possession, one of the defensive players from that team stepped over the restraining line. His team had possession and he was 20 yards behind the play, but he was on the side of the field where the coach whose team had committed the face off violation was positioned.

The coach began screaming at the top of his lungs and jumping up and down waving his arms yelling out "He left early, he left early, he left early". Our very experienced official who had just began play with the whistle turned to the bench and duplicated the coaches physical actions - jumping up and down and waving his arms while screaming back at the coach in the same tone of voice and volume as the coach had used "I don't care, I don't care, I don't care".

The parents attending the game roared with laughter and the coach turned bright red.

The ref who actually mirrored the coach and his crazy dance was John "Biz" Bistowski.

SHEEPISH TONY

SUBMITTED BY
BILL KELLY LACROSSE OFFICIAL

Towson is playing Syracuse @ Towson, Tony Seaman is coaching Towson and has been giving the officiating crew an earful, but never crossed the invisible line that would have resulted in either a conduct or unsportsmanlike conduct foul. I am in transition from the goal official to the trail official position and am following the play up the field on the bench side. As I cross the midfield line I look up and see Coach Seaman 10 yards on the field at the top of the offensive box. Thinking he is on the field yelling at a crew member or coaching the team 10 yards on the field I reach for my penalty flag. As I am about to loft the flag in the air Coach Seaman turns and sees me. He has the look of "a deer caught in the headlights", he quickly holds up my partners score card and yells…. he dropped it and I was picking it up for him!!! Fortunately, I was able to hold onto the flag and Tony handed me the dropped scorecard.

GETTING "HOMERED"

SUBMITTED BY
BILL KELLY, LACROSSE OFFICIAL

Catholic University (from Washington D.C.) was playing a game in the Baltimore area. The calls were going against Catholic and their coach was complaining that he always "gets homered" when he comes to Baltimore. As he made that statement the ball went out of bounds and I was in front of the Catholic University bench. As the players were substituting on a horn the coach from Catholic again stated he felt he was "getting homered". As play resumed I said to him "I don't want to hear any more about you getting homered…..the guy who just made the last 2 calls against your team is Catholic". A few moments later I was again by the coach who replied, "What did you say" I again told the coach the official who just made the 2 calls you didn't like is Catholic, and as a matter of fact all 3 officials on the game are Catholic!" Never heard another comment about Catholic U getting "homered" the rest of that game.

THE FIRST "HIGHLIGHT FILM"

SUBMITTED BY
CARL RUNK

In the coming week-end we would be playing the Frostburg State football team. Phil Albert and I, since we had the time, decided to scout Frostburg, located up in the far northwestern part of our state. We were totally unimpressed with the performance of the football team, graded them as a sub-par unit, and while driving home, we planned our strategy for the game. I recall telling Phil, "One thing we can't do is tell the team just how bad the Frostburg group was!" We had decided that this game would be a great opportunity to film our season highlights. I remember convincing the AD that the filming should be in color (more attractive but more expensive) and would be used for program promotion and recruiting purposes.

As the game started we were quick to learn that Frostburg was not as bad as we thought. Maybe we under estimated them. No maybes' about it!!.......we did!! This was a good football team and we were in a hell of a fight, trying to survive and at least save some of the equipment! They were beating the hell out of us. Frostburg had a defensive end who was 6'7" and massive. This Pro football candidate dominated the game. At one time during the game, after we had taken our starting quarterback out because of injury, we called on the services of our backup quarterback, Bobby Roche, a strong, intelligent, and highly capable athlete. At the start of play, Bobby dropped back to pass and was quickly hammered by that big defensive end. We called out to see if he were all right and, as he picked up his helmet, he waved his hand that everything was ok. The team broke from the huddle and took their positions, with Bobby pointing out the defensive alignment. He then set up to take the snap, but unfortunately, set up under the guard instead of the center. The guard, not used to having a pair of hands placed between his legs, surprisingly jumped while the center tried to signal to the quarterback to move over to him. To add insult to injury, the defensive team started yelling and laughing while pointing to the QB and taking "high fives"!! I looked at Phil and said "This is embarrassing! What else could go wrong?!!" It was at that time that Phil pointed to the top of the stadium where our film man was positioned. It seems something went wrong with the camera and the film sprung out and scattered all over the roof! The person doing the filming threw his hands up in disgust and was leaving the area. We chalked it up as a very, very bad experience.

So much for the highlight film that year!

RIGHT GAME ... WRONG BALL

MIKE MAHONEY
LAWRENCE UNIVERSITY

We were facing off against one of our league rivals RPI at home for the regular season conference championship. To give you some background, many of the coaches in the league are often apprehensive about the quality of officiating in Northern NY. I sometimes go to great lengths to assure them that they will be treated to a high level of officiating.

In this particular game, on the opening faceoff, St. Lawrence won the draw and our player attempted to move the ball to an attackman. As it turns out, the ball became lodged in his stick and he was unable to make the pass. Obviously the officials whistled the violation and awarded the ball to RPI. It was in the process of getting the ball out of our stick, that our player noticed they had actually faced off to start the game with a field hockey ball!! Not an easy mistake to make if you have ever compared a lacrosse ball to a field hockey ball!

Needless to say, the opposing coaching staff was not too impressed with this mistake, and the officiating crew may have lost a little credibility in the process. Fortunately things were quickly back in order and the Saints won the game on a last second goal!

SANTA BARBARA STREAKER

SUBMITTED BY
A CALIFORNIA OFFICIAL

The scene was a particularly close contest at UC Santa Barbara in front of about 500 fans. On this sunny spring Saturday, students had pulled out couches, lawn chairs, and blankets to enjoy the weather and the lacrosse action. At halftime of the game, with the officials in the table area having a rest and some water, the crowd suddenly let out a roar. A guy was riding on his mountain bike and circling the center of the field absolutely naked! When we stood up it caught his attention and he quickly departed the field with the crowd absolutely howling! UC Santa Barbara ended up winning that game and I always wondered if the streaking biker had any impact on the outcome.

PANTLESS GOALKEEPER

SUBMITTED BY
THE SAME CALIFORNIA OFFICIAL

Before a game at Cal Lutheran University on a sunny day with temperatures in the 90s, a player approached from behind and said, "Excuse me sir." I turned around and the goalie from the visiting team was standing there with his helmet and equipment all ready to play. He lamented on the heat and explained how uncomfortable his game shorts were in hot weather because they didn't allow him to breathe. He asked if he would be a penalized if he was not wearing game shorts like the rest of the team. I looked down and realized he was standing there in his boxers wearing his cup and jockstrap over a pair of colorful boxers. After realizing that his question was completely serious, I responded, "Son, I'd highly recommend that you wear your game shorts like the rest of the team today."

WHAT WAS I THINKING

SUBMITTED BY
NEAL PILTCH - MANZANO DAY SCHOOL OFFICIAL

I was officiating a high school game and one of the coaches, a person who was a great guy off the field but on the field always looked for ways to bust officials chops was not happy with my partner and had already been banged once by him. Things had finally settled down and the coaches' team was well in control in the 4th quarter. I was the trail and was near the box on the bench side when the coach said "Neal, I'm wondering if I can get flagged for what I am thinking" I think you know the rest of the story… I told him no, he could think whatever he wanted. As you can guess the next sentence started with "I am thinking that" and in a very quiet way let me know about his displeasure. All I could do is laugh. He wasn't trying to show anyone up nor was he really acting like a jerk. As the play went the other way I gave the coach a thumbs up and told him "he got me" but don't try it again!!

The other situation was in my early years of officiating and involved a men's club game. As we all know our job in a club game is to make sure nobody gets hurt. Early in the second quarter two teammates started to yell at each other about the quality of shot selection by one of the players who was a midfielder. The exchange ended with the promise to beat the sh— out of the player by his teammate if he took another similar to the ones he had taken. Sure enough on the team's next possession the midfielder took a shot from 5 yards beyond the restraining line which missed the cage by miles. The attack kept passion but before we could restart, the midfielder had been jumped by his teammate and they were having an all-out brawl. Nobody tried to break it up. Things finally settled down, and the problem became how to handle the situation. The consensus of both teams was to kick the midfielder out because he was embarrassing the game while letting his teammate go unpunished for upholding the game. (yes I am paraphrasing) Since it was a club game and I had the ability to keep virtually everyone happy that it was what we decided.

A "MCCALLISM"

SUBMITTED BY
TOM GILL HEAD COACH US COAST GUARD ACADEMY

While working with Fran Mcall at Bethpage I did my student teaching with him, his team was playing at Manhasset high school and things were not going very well, in his opinion, from the officiating end, I know John Goldsmith and Frenchy Julien were the officials, Coach Mccall took a time out huddled his team made some adjustments and then as they were going back out to the field coach turned around to the officials, facing the stands, bent over, grabbed his ankles and said to both refs "let me make this a lot easier for you"!!

DEDICATED FILM WATCHING

SUBMITTED BY
FRANK MEZZONATTI, FORMER ASSISTANT COACH, TOWSON UNIVERSITY

Frank Mezzonotti tells the story about a situation that happened at his summer camp in Rocks, Md. It seems there was a 13 year old youngster who convinced his dad to send him to camp. After the father agreed, the youngster asked if he could take the TV to camp with him so he could watch it in the evenings when there was nothing to do. The father, wanting the boy to have a great experience, agreed. The persistent youngster asked for permission to take the VCR player. Without hesitation, dad agreed. This was, without a doubt, a very happy camper! The father called Frank to see if it were all right to bring the TV and equipment to camp. He also said this was an exceptional youngster who will be a gem to have at camp.

On the second night of camp, according to the schedule, the kids were to come down to the pavilion to watch sports movies. This particular night not too many kids showed up for the film. Frank and a few of the coaches thought something must be wrong and decided to check things out. They decided to take a walk up to the cottages in the woods. As they approached one of the cottages they observed a large number of kids on the porch who, as soon as they saw the coaches coming, fled into the woods. The coaches, being a little concerned, opened the door to the cottage and walked in. To their surprise, they were stunned to see the room packed with youngsters watching porn films! It seems the industrious camper with the TV & VCR, this exceptional youngster, was charging $.50 a person for admission to the show!!

A livid Frank Mezzonnatti went storming through the room like a mad man, screaming at the kids, while confiscating the electrical appliances. He told the youngster, who by this time had wet his pants, that he was "out of here", and his father would be here in the morning to take him home.

Later in the evening, when things cooled down somewhat, Frank took a walk over to the coaches cottage, opened the door and ……..yeah, you got it!........The coaches had hooked up the equipment and were watching the films!! And there was no charge!!

WHAT COACHES WON'T DO TO WIN A GAME!!

SUBMITTED BY
CARL RUNK

The spring of '65 was a great year for Arizona lacrosse. We had a large number of returnees, a couple transfers, and some strong freshmen on the squad. Our contests were scattered from Northern Arizona, Southern California, Utah, to Colorado. A hell of a lot of travel, by station wagons, on a very limited travel budget, by the University, of $300!! Obviously, we had a few functions to raise funds which helped. Fortunately, we were too young to realize the hardship of travel. If I were 10 years older at the time, I would have suggested they "Stick It!!" Regardless, it was a super year with us going undefeated through the season, 11 wins and no losses. It was the final game of the year that really concerned me. We were to play the Air Force Academy in Tucson. We had already beaten them earlier in the season in Colorado Springs. On the day of the game I was in the locker room going through preparations. One of my responsibilities was to tape injuries, ankles, and anything needing taping.

As I was going through my duties, I heard one of the players exclaim "Oh-Oh, Coach is really going to be pissed when he sees you!!" I looked up to see our starting goalie, Barry Bingan, standing there with the biggest black eye you'll ever see! His eye was swollen shut! I immediately went into my second mood, outrageously livid!! "What the hell happened to you??" I shouted. "Coach, you're never going to believe this, but last night I went out with my girlfriend to a restaurant and got into a fight with this guy! I guess he got the better of me!" "He sure in hell did, Pal! How the hell are you going to play with one eye?" I quickly contacted the medical trainer responsible for our game and explained our dilemma. When he came to the locker room he made a suggestion to cut the swelling which would relieve the fluid and pressure. It would open the eyelid enough to give him better vision. I asked Barry if he would agree to doing that. Without hesitation, he agreed. The trainer was correct. It did give him a little sight from that eye, making his sight somewhat 3-dimensional. I gave him a pair of sunglasses to wear during the game so the opposing players could not see that his vision was impaired. Believe it or not, Barry played great and we were able to beat the Air Force for the second time and go on having an undefeated season. We awarded him the game ball and I told him he could have the sunglasses. I was good that way!!

I often think of that game and incident and think of how <u>crazy we were at the time to do such a thing!</u> Can you imagine what the response would be today if you attempted that? I'd be working at a toll booth on interstate 95!!

Barry called me recently and reminded me of that incident.

"Don't forget to put that story in your book, coach!!

HOUSE FOR SALE

SUBMITTED BY
TOM GILL COACH COAST GUARD ACADEMY

Henry Ciccarone the outstanding lacrosse coach at Johns Hopkins University was always a contender for the National Championship. One of his biggest rivals in the late '70 was Cornell University, coached by the legendary Richie Moran. These two were always barging heads in competition and always at each other's throat. It seemed whomever won the contest between the two schools would win the national title. This particular year, Hopkins would travel to Ithaca, New York to play the Cornell team. It was a hard fought battle between two outstanding teams with the end result in Cornell's favor. Chic, as he was known, was not a good loser. He was extremely competitive and took losses seriously. After the game, on the way home, Chic had the bus driver stop at a local hardware store to pick up something. No one on the bus knew what he was getting. When he boarded the bus with a package, he told the driver to go to a specific address. It was Richie Moran's house. Once the bus arrived, Chic got out with his package and went right to the front of the house. He then took the purchased material from the package. It was a "FOR SALE" sign. He then proceeded to hammer it into the ground on Richie's front lawn. He boarded the bus a happier and more satisfied man, and off he went to Baltimore.

    He was one of my favorites!

RECRUIT SEYMOUR PABLOGOTZ

SUBMITTED BY
JACK EMMER, HALL OF FAME MEMBER, FORMER U.S. MILITARY COACH

One Sept. morning in 1995 at West Point I opened the mail to find a recruiting letter from Coach Jamieson at Bucknell which was addressed to the West Point HS Lacrosse program asking for outstanding senior prospects for Bucknell. (In those days they didn't start recruiting seniors until they were seniors).

It had a recruiting postcard enclosed which I filled and returned. On it I listed this senior lacrosse prospect, Seymour Pablogotz, who I said badly wanted to go to Bucknell. I mentioned he had scored 120 points last spring as a junior attackman, was 6'3" tall and 235lbs., a straight 'A' student who had gotten 1550 on his SATs. I added that he was going to be heavily recruited so try to get in touch with him asap. I included the phone number of the Pablogotz' which was actually my home phone number.

I went home that night and told my wife, Joan, that if a Bucknell coach called and asked for Seymour to give the phone to me.

Sept., Oct., Nov., all went by and NO CALL. Finally, one winter night in Feb., Frank Fedoraka, Sid's asst. coach called and asked for Seymour. Joanie, sharp as she is, still remembered and handed me the phone.

Now I, as Mr. Pablogotz, gave poor Coach Fedoraka a rash of stuff along the lines of "this kid wanted to go to Bucknell, he scored 120 pts., 1550 SATs, etc., etc., and no one ever called----now he is upset at Bucknell and has lost interest. "Where the hell have you guys been?"

Frank Fedoraka was a little stunned but finally answered: …"we at Bucknell Lacrosse recruit alphabetically and we are just getting to the 'P's".

With that I ranted and raved and told him that I wanted to talk to the head coach the first thing the next morning.

The next morning came and Coach Jamieson called and I couldn't contain myself I was laughing so hard and I came clean. To this day when I see Frank Fedoraka I refer to him as Seymour and we have a good laugh.

BOB GUCWA ... THE REFEREE

SUBMITTED BY
MITCH TULLAI LACROSSE OFFICIAL / FOOTBALL COACH

As football coach at St. Paul's School, I tended to direct our teams as much as possible from the sidelines. Consequently, many times I found myself on the field and on innumerable occasions was reminded by the officials to refrain from coming out on the playing field.

One of the officials who reminded me of this many times was Bob Gucwa, who was known not only for his fine work as a referee, but also for his quick sense of humor.

After St. Paul's School honored me by naming the football field the "Martin D. Tullai Athletic Field", Bob was assigned to work a game for us. At halftime as his crew came to the bench, he said to me with a smile and a glint in his eye, "Hey, I want to congratulate you on the field being named in your honor, and I know why the school did it……….you were on the field more than the players!"

OFFICIATING AT NAVY

SUBMITTED BY
MITCH TULLAI LACROSSE OFFICIAL

With Virginia slated to play at Navy in Lacrosse as appointing authority, I assigned Fred Eisenbrandt, Bob Schlenger and myself to officiate this important contest.

Following our usual procedure, before the game we went to both coaches to get the names of their captains and perform other pre-game responsibilities.

As we approached the normally good natured and affable coach of Navy, Dick Slasza, I noticed he was somewhat upset. He looked at me rather grimly and said "Mitch, I don't know what to say, I don't understand." Taken aback, I said "What's the problem coach?" He replied "as you know, the coach of Virginia, Ace Adams, is a graduate of St. Paul's School. Fred Eisenbrandt has had two sons graduate from St. Paul's School. Bob Schlenger had a son graduate from St. Paul's School and you are a long-time teacher, football coach and administrator at St. Paul's School. It looks like the odds are against us." I was somewhat dumbfounded. This wasn't the congenial, friendly and hospitable coach I had known over the years. Feeling dismayed, I swallowed hard in expectation of further adverse comments. He then sternly looked at me for almost a minute – but slowly this sternness turned into a twinkling smile as he quipped, "Hey I got you guys, didn't I! You know I'm only kidding. This is probably the best crew working today. Thanks for being here, have a good game."

This was the real Dick Szlasa.

"NO CHECK-OFFS"

SUBMITTED BY
MITCH TULLAI FOOTBALL COACH

After coaching varsity football at St. Paul's School for over 40 years, I retired and then volunteered to work with Mark Reuss, who was directing the 8th grade football team. He assigned me to work with the offense. In our last game of the season against a friendly rival, we were in a commanding lead. Not wanting to embarrass our opponent by scoring again, Mark decided we would call only simple running plays – no passes. Even if the opportunity presented itself, the quarter back was not to call any "check-offs" which would lead to a score. So both he and I began yelling into our play-caller, "No check-offs! No check-offs!" Upon hearing this, as he strolled the sidelines taking pictures, Edward Brown, a respected member of the English Department, known for his whimsical sense of humor, quipped "Wow, what a group, they are not only known for football, but are familiar with Russian literature." Anton Pavlovich chekhov).

THE TOOTHLESS SITUATION

MICKEY-MILES UNIVERSITY OF ARIZONA

Actually, I do have a story that relates to the old school Psychology of "winning by intimidation".

It was mid seventy's and when I first started playing at the University of Arizona. Things were extremely different for the Sport. Heck, back in the day, "Wild and Crazy" was more than just a phrase, it was a reality. I had only played midfield one year in high school and that was in the early '60's when the game was played with wooden sticks including one cat-gut wall. I understand but no, no, no, get that vision out from between your ears, we didn't play in loincloth. This story was back in the day, but not quite that far back in the day.

When I arrived in Tucson in one of my primes (I like to think I hit new primes about every 10 years), 30 years old, I began playing with the Cats as an inexperienced defenseman. As a transplanted wise guy from New York, I figured until I could improve skills, I needed an edge. After some «Wild and Crazy» thoughts, I settled on a psychological formula that worked for me or at least got me through those days when everyone was younger and more experienced.

I wore knee high, multi-colored, argyle socks, usually with silver threads accentuating the diamonds. During our warm-ups, some of our soon to be combatants had quizzical expressions on their mugs. However, the psychological kicker was the evil use of dark candy wrappers to black out my upper front teeth. Not too many of us meatheads used mouth pieces back then. I think we preferred the goofy feeling brought on by a good solid grade 1 concussion, followed by post game refreshments as a kicker.

Reese peanut buttercup wrappers were the perfect «food» for me. The milk chocolate was delicious, the peanuts smooth and digestible, and, as a bonus, same as today, there were 2 to a package. Excellent, I could use one for the beginning of the game, swallow up a Reese cup of energy at halftime, and use that second wrapper for the start of the second half.

But let's get back to the beginning of the game. After the obligatory midfield line-up when the players headed to their respective areas on the field and before the zebra put the pea into action for the opening face-off, I'd briskly saunter over to the attackman that I was playing that game, poke him in the ribs with my long stick, and display a big smile showing no teeth. That's right, not too close so he could get a good look but the longer D-Stick provided me just enough distance.

I'd then get closer and turn my back to him announcing, "By the time this game's over, you're going to have less teeth then me" and walk away with an "OoohhhhhhhhhYeeeaaahhhhhh" ringing through his ear holes.

Some guys wouldn›t dare come near me for the rest of the game, and, of course, it didn›t matter much to "real Lacrosse players". Hell, they were missing their own teeth. The difference was they had come by the holes in their gums, honestly. But that›s how I survived using the current psychology of the era!

editors note: (I always thought Mickey was a little weird!!)

THROUGH A PLAYERS EYES

SUBMITTED BY
ED STEPHENSON TOWSON '88

TSU vs. Delaware (at Delaware 1986): The game was a one or two goal game in the second half, and it was hotly contested. Just after a face off, three one-on-one fights broke out. One at our offensive end of the field (Eddie Bollinger), one at the defensive end (I don't remember if it was Stefanides or Bruno?), and one at the midfield. I have never seen anything like that before; but that's not the funny thing. The funniest thing in the world was when Coach Runk went to turn to his left to keep everyone on the bench, all of us ran to his right! I was the last one that made it by Coach, and "Skinny" (Mark Moran), "Guido" (Mark Aguiri?), and I think, Mark Todd, players on the team, were all caught by coach's eyes (and halted immediately). The guys that made it by with me, although being in coach's view, didn't make eye contact with Coach Runk. It was a dilemma, we had too much respect for him to make eye contact (we knew if we did, we'd respect his demands, and stay). However, Delaware's bench was emptying, so most of us sprinted by to his right and kept our focus away from him. We laughed and retold the story for what seems like a hundred times.

Another funny thing, as the skirmishes broke out, and during the charge; Out of the corner of my eye, I saw "Weeder" (Carl Weedameier, a freshman "hillbilly' from Anne Arundel County) he only played for a year or two) run full speed toward the middle melee. He put his stick parallel to the ground at about 5 feet high, with his hands braced in the middle, and he took off into the air. He cleared out the entire group, ours and theirs. He was quite a character. You remember "Weeder", a big, bulky, 220 pound defender. His dad was a sheriff down in Anne Arundel County. We had some characters:

"Skinny" – Mark Moran. Also known as "Crazy" for the way his legs looked crazy when he ran.

"Grit" - Jason Levinson. The "Little Jew". Loved the outdoors, and country living.

"Guido" - Mark Aguire. Remember when we scrimmaged a team (I think it was Hobart in the spring, 1986), and Mark filmed it. Either he knew, or didn't know, that the camera audio was on, but either way, he made disparaging comments throughout the scrimmage (all were picked up on the film). When we watched film on Monday, Coach Runk allowed the film to play, with the audio on. Needless to say, Mark's time on the team was short-lived. That was the quietest film session ever! It is a lot funnier now than it was then.

TUCSON, THE HEALTH CAPITAL OF THE WORLD

SUBMITTED BY
CRAIG STARKEY, FOOTBALL '62

The football coaches at the University of Arizona took tremendous pride in their recruiting prowess. It could have been described as an aggressively competitive, "I recruited the best!!" type frenzy. They truly enjoyed expressing their recruiting successes, in a "ribbing" manner, to each other. Ron Marciniak was not an exception to the rule. His recruiting strategy, from the initial home visit to the school visit was strictly of a positive nature. He could just "over-nice" and "stroke" you to the extent you, as a player, felt completely satisfied, wanted and important.

The players enjoyed telling stories about how they were recruited by Coach Ron. One story that was consistent with the home visit was Ron telling the parents and the recruit that if you overslept, were late for class and/or missed your breakfast in the morning, you could very easily get your nourishment from any of the orange trees around campus. "Just take an orange or two from the trees and eat them on the way to class." What he failed to tell you was that the oranges were decorative, sour as hell, and for show only!!

I was always in awe at how many of the freshmen fell for that story and how half of them would run out of class to make a morning contribution in the men's room!

On visiting the school, Coach Ron would always tell the recruit "Tucson was the health capital of the world". That people with different health problems would come from all over the world to partake in the healthy dry environment Tucson has. "People just don't die here!!" Two players who experienced the "health capital" story shared the following story with me.

Coach Ron picked us up at the airport to take us to the University. On the way he would point out all the important points about the city he knew. Some were really trivial like "That's a McDonalds there on the corner where you can get something to eat in the evening!" or "there's a laundry mat if you need to clean your clothes!" Things of real importance!

As we were driving down the street we saw a funeral procession coming toward us. I said to coach, "Coach, I thought you said Tucson was the health capital of the world and nobody dies here !! Ron answered "It is!!" Then I said "What about this funeral procession coming towards us?" Ron quickly and without hesitation, responded, "Yeah, that's the funeral director. Paper said he starved to death!!!"

THE BEE STING

SUBMITTED BY
CARL RUNK

We were involved in football two-a-days in the middle of August on a miserable hot humid day. As practice progressed, an outstanding athlete and fullback came running to me in a fearful and highly concerned manner.

"Coach Runk!! I've got to go to the locker room!!" I answered "what's the problem?" He responded in a very frightened way, "Coach, I am allergic to bee stings and I just got stung by a bee!! If I don't get my medication in 10 seconds I could die!!!" I quickly told him to "get out of here and get your medication!" He took off in a hard sprint. I guess I watched him for a few seconds when Coach Albert hurriedly came over to ask me if everything was ok. I said to Albert, "Phil, how far are we from the locker room? He responded, "A little over 2 hundred yards!! Why?" I said, "Well, in just a few seconds we're going to witness one of two extraordinary events. Either a world record in the 100 dash or a terrible disaster!!"

Fortunately, the youngster received the medication he needed and there was no disaster!

SHOULD YOU TELL THE TRUTH?

SUBMITTED BY
CARL RUNK

A very good friend of mine, throughout his life, was always involved with sports as a player, coach or affiliate of some sort. Because of his athletic prowess, I knew of him long before our friendship developed. As a young athlete in high school I was always thrilled to have this well respected individual approach me in his friendly way offering encouragement and advice. He made me feel special. This individual became a legend in Baltimore, especially in the east side of town. In his later years, like many of us, he became ill, worried a great deal about the illness, and was taken to the hospital. He literally thought this was his time and he would be moving on soon.

With his entire family gathered around him at the hospital, he asked that he could visit with his wife alone. It was at this emotional time he poured his heart out to his wife telling her about his escapades with other females and asked for her forgiveness. He wanted to relieve himself of all his wrongdoing before he left this earth. It was also at this emotional time that the doctor walked in the room and exclaimed, "Sir, we have good news for you! You will be released from the hospital tomorrow morning. You're free to go home!! The diagnoses showed that you only had some kind of intestinal inflammation!"

The next day, after his release from the hospital and on his arrival home he found all of his belongings neatly packed, on the front porch of his house! My friend lived many, many years after that episode……but, unfortunately, not at home with his wife!

BATHROOM LEAKAGE

SUBMITTED BY
CARL RUNK

Tom Hayes, well known Lacrosse Hall of Fame inductee, former lacrosse coach at Rutgers University, and presently retired, has an enviable life-style at this time. Like many retirees, Tom shares his winter months in Marco Island, Florida. Since I also, have a small place in Naples, Florida and heard that Tom was in close vicinity, I felt I'd give him a call and maybe we could get together for lunch. In typical "Runk" fashion I thought I would have some fun with him. I called him on the phone telling him this was a call from the Marco Island Plumbing Service and we had some complaints about his bathroom toilet, that the occupants in the condominium below were complaining about water damage to their bedroom furnishing. I mentioned that evidently he had a leakage in his bathroom toilet and every time he flushed the toilet it caused water problems for his neighbor. I told him we were on our way to his condominium to fix the problem and that he should have a check available for services rendered. "Wait a minute, we are renting this condo, we don't own it!! I exclaimed, "It doesn't matter, according to the Florida rental regulations, whoever is in the condo at the time of the problem, owner or lessee, is responsible for the payment. Tom almost had conniptions!! At this point, I couldn't go any further without laughing out loud. I told him that it was me calling and I was only playing with him. After a few choice words, we both enjoyed the story and later in the day had lunch together………which he paid!

LOU WHO??

SUBMITTED BY
KEVIN CORRIGAN LACROSSE COACH NOTRE DAME UNIVERSITY

My first practice in the fall of 1988 at Notre Dame I was surprised to find that we were on a field adjacent to the football practice field and more surprised there was no fence between the two fields. We did everything we could to keep balls from going onto their field, but there was no way to keep them off completely. I kept an eye on Coach Holtz as balls would occasionally spill over to their practice, and was horrified when about a half hour in Coach jumped in his golf cart and headed towards me. He pulled up and asked me, "Kevin, do you have any Irishmen on this team?" I wasn't sure what to think but I replied, "Yeah Coach, we have Kevin O'Connor and Eamon McAnaney and a bunch of others, why?" Without missing a beat he says, "Christ, there ought to be a law against giving a stick to an Irishman". And with that he jumped into his golf cart and drove away. I still think it was his way of letting me know he saw all the balls coming into his practice…but it was a funny way to let me know.

ANOTHER STORY

SUBMITTED BY
KEVIN CORRIGAN LACROSSE COACH NOTRE DAME UNIVERSITY

My first year at Notre Dame we were hoping to make some changes…upgrade the schedule, increase our profile for recruiting, etc…just trying to make some kind of splash. One of the biggest things was we had Johns Hopkins come out to play us in the fall. They had just won the 1987 national championship, so it was a big deal to have them here to play us. Now this was the 1988 fall football season, which if you remember was the year Notre Dame won the National Championship. The forecast was for bad weather, so in anticipation of bad weather I went to Coach Holtz and asked him if we could use the Loftus Center, our indoor field, as a backup site.

    Now at that time, the football team's custom on Friday evenings was to go to the Pep rally on campus and then come back to the Loftus Center where they would turn out all the lights and the players would lie spread out on the turf in the dark and Coach Holtz would talk to them and do some mental imagery stuff to relax them and prepare them for the game the next day. Coach couldn't have been more gracious, said he thought it was great that we had a chance to play the defending champions and wished us luck.

Friday night comes and the weather is awful, so we move inside. Half way through the third quarter I get a tap on my shoulder and it is George Kelly. George was a longtime assistant football coach at ND who was now Lou's administrative aid. Coach Kelly says to me "OK Kev, we're here now and it's time to go". I was dumbfounded, and said to him, "Coach, I spoke with Lou and he said we were good to go". George says, "I don't know what you guys said, but he is outside that door right now with the whole team and they are ready to come in and do our thing before we go to the hotel." I said "see if you can talk to him…and at least buy us some time", and he left. I figured we were getting killed anyway and we could go to running time or something.

Ten minutes later Coach Kelly is back and he says "I did everything I could, but now you have to go." Well now I'm kind of pissed, so I say to George "we're playing a game here…and on top of that we're trying to make a statement about lacrosse at Notre Dame, and if we quit now and leave so you guys can come in here to lay in the dark , well… that's not the statement we're trying to make". I tell him, "George, this is my first game at Notre Dame, and it may be my last, but we can't quit in the middle of the game" and with that I turn around and go back to the game. I tell the box to make it running time, and coach the rest of the game with one eye on the door and scared to death that the next tap on my shoulder will be Coach Holtz.

Amazingly we finish the game and I never hear another word about it that night. Of course on Monday I'm scared to death every time the phone rings that it is going to be the AD telling me that we're dropping lacrosse. That afternoon Mike Brennan, a great high school lacrosse player from Baltimore who had walked on to the football team four years earlier, stopped by my office. Mike was now

Another Story

a starter on the football team and apparently a guy with some juice. He told me that when Coach Kelly had told Coach Holtz that we were still on the field that night he had overheard what was going on and had intervened on our behalf, telling Coach Holtz that it was a huge deal for us and suggesting that they could do their session at the hotel instead. Thankfully Coach Holtz agreed…and since they won the next day to remain undefeated we lived to fight another day.

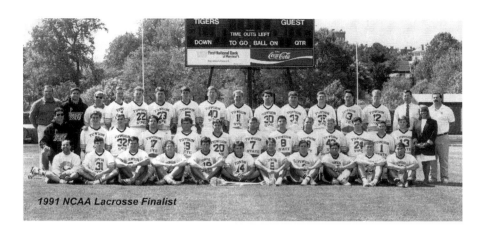

1991 NCAA Lacrosse Finalist

J. D. DAVIS

SUBMITTED BY
CARL RUNK

Besides being an honorable profession, coaching quite often allows the coach to play a role in a number of positive and lifelong player experiences. Some time during the course of the season he has the opportunity to witness a youngster engaging in an extraordinary effort of physical performance. This youngster, for some reason, rises above his past level of play to perform at a higher level. He "rises to the occasion!" He does something he has never done before. What a rewarding experience this is for both player and coach.

I have, in my tenure, seen this happen quite often but one experience comes to mind whenever this topic is discussed.

In the late 70's we had a highly respected team but the team dominating the Division II world was Roanoke College. The coach of that team was Paul Griffin, an outstanding young coach who was a credit to the game of lacrosse. Paul left the coaching profession to fulfill his lifelong quest of becoming an administrator in athletics. He is, at this writing, the Senior Associate Athletic Director at Georgia Tech. While at Roanoke College Paul was experiencing an undefeated season with one game remaining on his schedule. It was the Towson University team he would have to beat to achieve the "golden ring".

    The practices we had the week of the game were outstanding with each and every player looking forward to the game with Roanoke. After our last practice, back in the office, I met with the coaches and told them of my decision to start a youngster, a senior, who had little game time experience but for the past four years was a catalyst for winning on our team. J.D. Davis was a highly respected player who was revered by his teammates. He was a devoted athlete for our institution, participating in cross-country along with lacrosse. He had the ability to run strong and consistently throughout a practice or contest as if he had three lungs! He was in superb shape and he deserved the opportunity to start. He had given me four years of outstanding effort and never once complained about playing time. The coaching staff thought this was an excellent idea and it was decided that J.D. and team would be told prior to the game the next day. At our pre-game meeting I told the team of my decision to start J.D. I thought his eyes were going to pop out. He was really excited as was the team. And what an uplifting experience!! He performed with the first midfield like he's been there all year. And what a game he had!! J.D. was over every ground ball, contributed with a few assists, rode tenaciously, and even scored. He gave our kids the momentum to dominate the game and not allow Roanoke the distinction of having an undefeated season. He "rose to the occasion"! And we loved him for it!!

    After the contest, in the middle of the field, I spoke with Paul Griffin. He congratulated me on the effort our kids put forth and then asked, "Coach, were the hell did you get that number 27?" We scouted your team the last two games and didn't know anything about him. That kid practically beat us by himself!! What an effort he put out!!!" Trying to sound like I knew what I was talking about, I sheepishly told him "Oh, you're talking about J.D. Davis…..Well, he's been injured most of the season and we just got permission to play him today!!"

Sometimes I wish I would have given J.D. a chance to start a lot earlier in the season. I might have been a better coach!

A SLUG OF MOUTHWASH

SUBMITTED BY
JIM AMEN FORMER COLLEGE & HIGH SCHOOL COACH LONG ISLAND DISTRICT ATHLETIC COORDINATOR

I first got to Johns Hopkins University in 1977.

Bob Scott and Henry Ciccarone (may he rest in peace) hired me as assistant lacrosse coach and head men's basketball coach. Each fall Scotty would meet with the incoming freshman students at some gathering …. something to do with new student freshman orientation. I remember getting ready to attend with scotty and as I walked out of my office with chic /// I was standing outside of Scotty's office and as I looked in, Scotty was taking a slug of something out of a bottle … Me, being a newcomer … I was stunned … was this Bob Scott taking a drink before addressing the students … Chic was laughing (as usual) I said "Chic what is Scotty doing??" Chic, still laughing, said to me … "He is gargling with mouthwash!!" I should have known better!!

AN ANXIOUS YOUNG COACH

SUBMITTED BY
JIM AMEN

We were playing Coach Runk's team at Towson and me, being the new guy on the block was very careful of my role. The 1st half ended and we headed up the hill to the locker room … A long, long walk! … I told Fred Smith (may he rest in peace, also) that I had my watch set for the tradional period of time for a time out so we would not be penalized for delay of game. As half time winded down, I told Freddie that we had about two minutes to wrap it up. We left the locker room a short time afterwards and the next thing I know Mitch Tullai, the official, is giving us a 30 second penalty for delay of game and he and Chic are going at it!! I knew that we were not late as I had the time on my watch … I sort of went over to where Chic and Mitch were going at it and said …Mr. Tullai … I had the time on my watch … we were not late … The next thing I knew Coach Chic was yelling at me to mind my own business and he would handle it himself . Perhaps not funny, but I was scared to death!! Anyway, as always, Chic later apologized to me …

No harm…No foul!

Just a loyal young assistant trying to do his best!

3 IN 1 OIL

SUBMITTED BY
CHARLES JURIS HEAD COACH BACK BAY LACROSSE CLUB PORTLAND MAINE (MANY YEARS AGO!)

First day of practice in a brand new season. Weather required the team to report to the gym for the first day and as players entered the gym, myself and my first assistant greeted the players, asking if they were all set and ready for what was about to begin? A great day for every high school lacrosse team. As the players filed through the line saying hello, we had typical requests like, coach I forgot my stick at home, do we need our equipment today, do not have my forms, what time will practice be over, typical lacrosse questions that we have all suffered through and had to answer with coaches concern and then in some cases with humor.

As the line proceeds a young man comes before the two coaches and asks, "Coach, do you have any 3 in 1 oil"? The coaches look at one another, immediately start patting down our pockets and then look at the player with broad smiles on our faces and report, "Sorry we guess we are fresh out of 3 in 1 oil" The player, taken with our effort to search ourselves on his behalf thanks us with all seriousness and proceeds toward the gym.

After more than 20 years combined coaching experience, we had to ask the player as he walked away, "Hey, son, what exactly does a lacrosse player need with 3 in 1 oil on the first day of practice." The player responds over his shoulder, "Oh Coach, my knee brace is squeaking" Coaches crack up and comment to each other, that was a first.

And now after more than 30 years in the game that was the only time we have ever had a request for 3 in 1 oil.

Sorry I went out and bought a can a long time ago! What a waste of money!!

Great memories, simple, but it's what makes the kids and the game wonderful.

THE HOAGIE EATER

SUBMITTED BY
WAYNE JAECKLE LACROSSE COACH WASHINGTON UNIVERSITY IN ST LOUIS

My name is Wayne Jaeckle and I was the head varsity coach at Seneca Valley HS in Pittsburgh Pa. I was also president of US Lacrosse Pittsburgh chapter when Coach Runk came to speak at our end of year banquet around 2003. We had a top 5 team back in 2004 and had a real good goalie who went on to play in college. His back up was Mike Hockenberger who was sort of the team clown and was a little overweight and out of shape. Well our top goalie took a personal penalty and we needed the backup to go in so I call for Mike and look over at him and he's sitting on the bench eating a hoagie sandwich. He proceeds to shove the hoagie up under his chest protector and waddle into the game, plays for a minute and when the penalty is served he comes back out pulls the hoagie out and finishes eating it.

This same player also told me once in practice the first few weeks coaching him that he missed practice because his mother had died! I met her 2 weeks later! One funny kid!!

THE COCONUT PIE

SUBMITTED BY
DAVE WILSON DETROIT CATHOLIC CENTRAL LACROSSE

In 2008 my assistant's, Jon Sullivan, birthday fell on a practice day. His nephew was a captain and Jack wanted to squish a pie in his face to mark the occasion. I devised a plan to stall for time at the end of practice meeting that we have on the field. Jack got the pie and snuck around Jon who was delivering a coaching gem about hard work and not screwing around at practice. Jack nailed coach square in the kisser with a nice coconut cream pie and it splattered all over the place including his brand new cold weather gear coachs' jacket! Needless to say it was named Jacks favorite moment of the season at senior night over the p.a. system. We still laugh about it from time to time!

SPECIAL PLAYS WORK

SUBMITTED BY
CARL RUNK

Sometimes we, as coaches, love to get a benefit or "gift" in a ball game that we really don't deserve. It may be an official not seeing the whole picture or a "call" that shouldn't have gone our way. But if it's to our advantage …… well, we'll take it anyway and without remorse.

Prior to a ball game, at the meeting with the officials, I would usually point out a special play technique they should know about that we would use in certain situations of the game.

The Situation: We are a man-down, clearing the ball from the back line. Our short stick, with the ball, will run towards the crease having the riding defender putting pressure on him. Since the defender is between the ball carrier and the crease, we want our ball carrier to go as close to the crease as possible on a sprint. Hopefully, the defender playing the ball with great intensity, would not observe the crease and step into the crease illegally, therefore giving us a free clear.

I can't begin to tell you how many times that situation came about and we got the call in our favor. And after viewing the film we realized, quite often, the defender was not in the crease and that the official just rushed his judgement. But it was to our benefit ….. So what the hell!!

PLAYING WITH THE OFFICIAL

SUBMITTED BY
CARL RUNK

We had one official, no name given, that we would take advantage of during the course of the game. With the opposing team clearing the ball on a fast clear, as the trail official would pass our bench near the mid-line, I would shout out, "It worked Coach!! We got em!! Their off-sides!!!" And would you believe that little official, hearing us call that out, thinking he missed the call, would automatically blow his whistle signaling off-sides, giving the ball back to us! It didn't matter what the opposing coach would say, the official would not make a change in his call. I used to love to make this call any time we played a "Cottle" (Loyola)) coached team just to hear the coach, Dave Cottle, go out of his mind, ranting and raving but to no avail!!

"Old Chinese Philosophy"

"Sometimes it is necessary to use any and all moves available, at the time, to advance your program."

"Old Runk Philosophy"

I don't know of too many Chinese playing lacrosse!!!

THE OFFICIAL LOOK-ALIKES

SUBMITTED BY
CARL RUNK

How many times have you mistaken one person for another. I've done it a number of times but one time that stands out was when it involved lacrosse officials.

It seems there were two officials that looked so much alike I really thought they were the same person! And I would always refer to them, whenever I saw them, as "Vinnie". Even though I would make this mistake time and time again, 50 % of the time I was correct!

In 1995 Towson would be competing against Syracuse. At the pre-game introduction of officials, Tom Young, the chief official, came to me in the middle of the field to go over regulations and any questions I may have. He started by introducing me to his crew. "Coach Runk, you know Vinny Rosso …. and our other official is Mike Ventura". I believe I stood there, quite surprised, for a few seconds scratching my head and remarked "Got Dang!!!! There are two of you!!" It was hard enough for me to remember the names of the kids on my team let alone trying to remember two spaghetti stuffed Italian referee look-a-likes!! To this day, if I should bump into either one of the two, I'll address them as "Vinnie." Fortunately for me, they understand and respond in a positive manner!

YOUR RESPONSIBLE FOR YOUR OWN SET-UPS & BREAK-DOWNS

SUBMITTED BY
CARL RUNK

The football season was coming to an end and we needed one more win to call it a "very successful season!" Our next opponent was Shepard College, a team approximately one and a half hours from Towson. On the morning of the game we had a hell-of-a snow storm. Phil Albert & I were in the office early going over game details and wondering if we were going to get the game played. It was at that time the phone rang with the opposing coach on the other end. "Coach, how the hell is the weather down there? We've got a blizzard up here and I'm not sure we'll be able to play." "I don't want to come all the way down to your place and have to turn around and go back." I'll never know why I told him we were ok ….. It wasn't snowing and we could play the game, but I did. Maybe I just wanted to win that game and end the season. Since the support staff, an equipment man, didn't get paid for coming in on Saturdays or Sunday to support, it was up to Phil Albert and I to get the shovels and go down to the field and start shoveling. We started with the goal lines trying to clear an area of three feet on each side. With no place to throw the snow, the only place to throw each shovel full was in the end zone. The next area was the sidelines. Eventually, our players came out and at that point we had everybody shoveling. About an hour and 30 minutes before the start of the game the opposing team showed up. Phil and I were shoveling the three yard extra point area in sweat soaked t-shirts when the Shepard coach came up to us and exclaimed "Where's the dumb son-of-a-b____ that coaches this team?!!!" Leaning on my shovel, I looked over to him and said I was that coach. He responded, "Coach, I thought you said the field was in good shape?" I told him we were supposed to play in the stadium but the administration said because of the conditions, we would have to play on this practice field. (It's important to know we <u>did not</u> have a stadium field and the field we were shoveling <u>was</u> our home field!!) Being a little upset, the Shepard coach asked where the dressing room was. He also stated his team would not warm up on "this" field. They would come from the bus to play the game. For some reason, I kept getting into this mess deeper and deeper.

The game wasn't anything to write home about!! It was a time when the rushing game dominated the throwing game. Sometime during the 3rd quarter Shepard ran a sweep. Our players stopped pursuing the ball because they thought the Shepard running-back was out of bounds. The line judge wasn't sure where the ball was and called it a touchdown. We tried to convince him it was the wrong call … we even showed him the running backs football prints in the snow! He wouldn't go for it. With the addition of the extra point the score was 7 to 0.

Near the end of the game with just a minute of playing time, we were able to score. It was my decision to kick the extra point. The players lined up for the play.

Your Responsible For Your Own Set-ups & Break-downs

Unfortunately, our center snapped the ball erratically, with the ball going high and past the holders' grasp, landing in the gut of the kicker. The kicker was so surprised he just grabbed onto the ball and started to run around the end. He was stopped about 1 foot from the goal line!!! The game ended 7 to 6, with no shaking of the hands….just running to the bus and to the dressing room. Obviously, our two man staff, both Phil and I, were devastated! This was a tough loss to accept.

On the following Monday I received a phone call from the vice-president of the university. He congratulated our team on an outstanding effort. He then proceeded to tell me how proud he was of both Phil and I. He said "There wasn't one person in the stands that believed we were going to go for two with the fake kick and end run! You really made a great call at that time!! You were way ahead of all of us!!!" Never one to not take advantage of a good opportunity, I responded, "We thought we might catch them off guard and it would have been a great call if we had scored."

Shortly after that, we received a message from the maintenance man, who, as I mentioned before, didn't work on the weekends, stating "Any time you use my shovels … please make sure you put them back correctly!!!"

Sometimes when your attacked …. they show no mercy … your attacked from all angles!!

POT IN A SOCK

SUBMITTED BY
CARL RUNK

Some years ago at the *Top Star Lacrosse Camp*, Hank came to me regarding a concern he had. He had received a envelope type package in the mail addressed to the camp. Therefore, he thought it was his and he proceeded to open it up. On the inside was a sweat sock that contained marijuana cigarettes. Hank quickly looked to the address again and noticed it was directed to a youngster at the camp. He asked me how we should proceed. I told Hank that because of the mail traveling across state lines, I was sure it was a federal offense and he should contact the director of athletics. We wanted to use the proper protocol in this matter. After being informed about the incident, the athletic director contacted the federal authorities, who in turn told him they would not proceed because the affair was too small and they were busy with larger, more important matters. He was told that the ingredients should be destroyed, after which it was.

Word got out on this occurrence and on the final day, before going home, two coaches, who came to camp together, approached us and wanted to know what was going to be done with the cigarettes. They offered to "take them off your hands and discard them on the way home!!" They also said, "you know….driving as far as we have to can be very boring and your gift could make the trip a lot more pleasant and make it go by a lot faster!!" Obviously, since we destroyed the cigarettes we had nothing to contribute. We wouldn't have given the coaches anything if we had it!! But they sure surprised me.

 Had I known they were going to ask for the substance I would have made something similar looking and given it to them. Just to see their facial expression when they got involved.

SIZE 13 PEP TALK

SUBMITTED BY
CHARLES GROSS TOWSON '71

During the 1971 season Towson's first game was home against Hobart. They had an indoor field house, didn't miss a practice and were quite ready for Towson. At half time it was 8-4 (Hobart winning). Coach Runk took the entire team to midfield and shared that he was going to plant "size 13" up a dark place in our body cavity if we kept playing as bad as we were. Frank Mezzanotti, a defenseman, asked for a «clarification» and that got us to loosen-up. We won 11-10 in overtime. Some beautiful memories.

WHAT WE REMEMBER ABOUT CERTAIN GAMES

SUBMITTED BY
MIKE LAFFERTY, CMAA ATHLETIC DIRECTOR DULANEY HIGH SCHOOL TOWSON CLASS OF 74'

It is very early spring of 73 (maybe 74). It is cold as hell and we are scrimmaging Maryland at College Park. Most of us are heavily dressed in sweat pants and long shirts to keep the cold out. The scrimmage is going well (who can remember scores?) and there are tons of Towson and Maryland fans all along the side lines of the practice field outside the stadium. Spectators are even right up behind our team bench. I'm the 4th defenseman and standing on the side line freezing my tail off when all of a sudden Coach Runk yells out, "Lafferty get the hell in there!!" At that point I'm so excited to get out there (Coach had way of making us respond quickly) that I didn't even bother to take my gloves off before grabbing my sweat pants at the legs and giving a hard yank to remove them. Right at that moment Coach looks over at me, looks away, looks back and says "Son, you gotta get yourself together". That was when I realized that my game shorts went down with my sweats to my knees and I'm standing there literally in my jock and practice jersey. Of course Coach took it in stride, me standing there in my jock with all these people around, he waited a moment and then just kind of quietly laughed. I pulled my shorts back up and ran on to the field. Can't remember what he yelled to me at that time but I'm sure it was some form of flattery while referring to me as a "pencil neck" or "son of a buck". To this day I can't remember a thing about the scrimmage or most games, except for that experience at Maryland with Coach. I guarantee you, he remembers it.

Another experience was in '73 at Catonsville Community College playing in a spring Hero's Lacrosse Tournament with Maryland Lacrosse Club and some other teams. We may have again been playing UM but I'm not certain. What I am certain of is how Coach had a way of getting the team motivated when we needed it.

We must not have been winning or playing very well. Coach calls a time out and tells us all to gather around him. We see that he is not too pleased and we are slow and reluctant to get too close to him. He yells "get in here" while at the same time grabs the face masks of the two nearest defensemen; Sal Mafi and Frank Mezzanotti. Coach starts banging the face masks of these two guys like they were puppets while yelling at how poorly we were playing. Coach's veins are popped out in his neck as he lifts these guys off the ground. You can be sure that there were many us that feared what could be next. Of course Sal and Frank went out and played like crazy guys (they were most of the time anyway). The team responded and we played respectively for the remainder of the game. At least that is what I remember. Many of us went out that night and could not stop talking about seeing Coach so intense and passionate.

Coach Runk was always kind and complementary to us when not at a game. I never had a coach that could motivate me to the extent that Coach Runk could. Furthermore, he was always a gentlemen and classy. No one could ever tell stories or entertain you like he could. He will always be "Towson Lacrosse". I have never forgotten the experiences. They were great.

A SECOND CHANCE

SUBMITTED BY
**JERRY BARATTA
TOWSON LACROSSE**

My senior year Coach Runk wanted to speak to me. Why? I was a knucklehead at times (probably a real pain in the butt). I had missed the bus for the first game of the year against Villanova. Hindsight, this affected the outcome of my career as I am in the all-time Towson record book for face-offs for the year and career. My replacement won 14 out of 20 face-offs. Why did I miss the bus. I went out the night before the game, got home late and when my alarm went off my roommate came into my room, shut off my alarm clock and left me there sleeping. After the team came back from Villanova, I was waiting outside of Coach's office. Coach called me into the office, I can't remember who was in the room with him as I was scared to death. Now remember, I was 6'1" 225 lbs of solid muscle and a real tough kid. Yes, scared to death. So Coach said "Beretta come in here". Now my name was Baratta (Ba-Rot- ta) but coach called me Beretta from the TV show. In the middle of the conversation, coach said Beretta, leave the room so we can talk behind your back. I just stared into space not understanding what coach was asking of me. So he said it again. Beretta, step out so we can talk behind your back. I still stared. He got up and said, "Beretta, get out". I immediately got up and got out. I paced outside the door trying to listen and then the door open. Coach said "Come in Beretta, I'm going to give you one more chance." I almost cried. It was one of those moments that changed my life forever. I worked harder and knew that life sometimes does not afford you multiple opportunities. I was blessed to have a second chance and I was not going to blow it. Thanks Coach Runk,

PRE-GAME MEAL

SUBMITTED BY
JOHN GRUBB TOWSON '68
HEAD COACH NORTH HARFORD HIGH SCHOOL

In 1967 when I was a freshman we were traveling to play Drexel. We stopped for lunch on the way up 95. Coach Runk gave each of us $5.00 to buy lunch. This was my first road trip and 5.00 was a lot of money back then. All I had to live on was 40.00 a month social security from when my father passed away. It was the end of the month and my funds were tight and all I could think of was getting a fulfilling meal. I was sitting next to Larry Gross, and he was from Long Island and that Italian culture from up there, so he said let's order spaghetti and meatballs in a red sauce....I thought that would be a good meal to stick to my bones for a while, so we did and ate it all with lots of Italian bread and butter.. We got back on the bus and arrived at Drexel and were getting dressed in the locker room when coach came up and told Larry and I he wanted to meet us outside with all our stuff on. So we got dressed and went outside and he took us on the field and lined us up on the end line and started blowing his whistle and making us run sprints. Coach Runk ran our butts off and we had a league game in 45 minutes so we could not figure out what was happening. After what seemed like an hour of this I felt that red sauce coming up real fast and soon I had noodles, etc., hanging off my face mask. Coach told us to stop running and came up to us and said "spaghetti is not what he considered a pre-game training meal on your dollar". I can tell you I never order spaghetti again when we were on the road with Coach.

ROOKIE PLANE TRIP

SUBMITTED BY
MARK THERIAULT KEENE COLLEGE

When I was playing for the Boston Blazers, the veteran players would go into the lavatory of the airplane and grab some "feminine napkins" While walking off the plane, the veterans would pat the rookies back giving them the "Glad you are here and good luck" line while, at the same time, sticking the napkins on them. The goal was to get as many on his back without him finding out. The best part was watching other passengers staring and laughing at them while walking through the airport to get their luggage/equipment.

THE WRONG RONNIE

SUBMITTED BY
CARL RUNK

Ron O'Leary was a longtime outstanding lacrosse official calling many of the most important games of his day. He had been in the game for many years and was revered by fellow officials and coaches. If he worked your game, you were very fortunate. One of the familiar traits that Ron had was he was highly sensitive to any coaching objections that came from the sideline. He did not hesitate to let you know how he felt about the situation. This would be accomplished in a calm way or, more than likely, in an aggressive manner with both arms flaring! But the coach knew where he, Ron, stood on the situation.

We were playing Maryland in a nail-biter at home, with Ron as the head official. Somewhere in the 3rd quarter our assistant coach, Jeff Clark, was screaming at one of our defenders on the field about missing his assignment. Unfortunately, the players' name was Ron. Jeff aggressively called out, "Ronnie, you're blowing it! You're losing it for us. Get your game together." Evidently our sensitive ear official, Ron, had taken enough! He turned and quickly made his way toward the timers box, looking like he was going to punch Jeff out and exclaiming in a volatile manner "That's it!! I've taken enough of your bull-crap!! I'm not going to stand for that bull crap anymore!!" He then proceeded to give us a one minute unsportsman-like penalty and told Jeff if he said another word he would personally throw him out of the stadium! I rushed out to him and tried to explain the situation. "Ronnie, he's not yelling at you…he's screaming at that dumb defensive player! His name is Ronnie also." There was a short quite period, a few seconds, and then he got up close to me and very quietly responded "Coach, I'm sorry, I guess I over-reacted. But I'm not changing the call .. …It would make me look bad!!" If I can help you later I will!!" He then turned and ran back onto the field. Fortunately, Maryland was not able to take advantage of the situation at that time.

You had to love Ron. He was one of the best!! His son Kevin, at this time, is following in his dad's shoes. He also is an outstanding lacrosse official. But there will never be another Ron O'Leary!

THE SWIMMING POOL INCIDENT

SUBMITTED BY
CARL RUNK

When I first arrived at Towson University I was fortunate to have my office in a brand new building, Burdick Hall, a state of the arts facility. This beautiful arena was home to athletics, health, dance and physical education which helped us tremendously in recruiting. We derived great pleasure and pride in showing the recruits around Burdick and bumping into health, physical education, and dance instructors, trying our best to be highly impressive. We took great pride in the "family" group impression we displayed. The building also housed an up to date large swimming pool with observation windows (4) on the bottom floor. This area was used as a teaching and coaching tool.

We had just finished our fall ball workout on an extremely hot afternoon. I was seated in my office when I was approached by the assistant coach and team captains regarding the possibility of the players using the swimming pool to cool off. I responded that they could not use the pool as it was not officially dedicated yet and, besides, the area was locked up anyway. The players told me the area was opened and the whole team was already partaking in the "cooling" process. Being a little concerned, I told the assistant coach to get down there and get them out of the pool before someone sees them and "all hell breaks loose!" Too Late!!! The swimming coach came through my office door screaming! "Those damm lacrosse players!! Their all over the pool and not one of them has any clothes or swim suit on!!"

He proceeded to tell me he was in the process of showing state dignitaries around, including the county executive, unfortunately a woman. They were down in the observation area when the county executive, unfortunately a woman, looking through one of the windows wanted to know "If the pool isn't dedicated yet…what are all those naked boys doing in it!!!" One thing for sure….They weren't trolling for alligators!!" The swimming coach was really upset and exclaimed he would make sure I received a letter of reprimand that would go into my personal file. (Like I give a damn!!) Some people just don't have a sense of humor!! And I'm willing to wager the county executive, unfortunately a woman, had mixed emotions about the whole thing!!

ANOTHER TIME

SUBMITTED BY
CARL RUNK

When showing the recruits around, we would always, before going to lunch or dinner, stop by the observation area as a last stop. We were in that area with some recruits. The only other person down there with us was a gentleman who was employed by the gas & electric company doing his work. On our way out of the observation area, I said, in a very kidding and joking manner, "You know….when the Maryland Nudist Society holds the nudist swimming championships … …You can't get a ticket to get in here!!! This place is packed!!!" The kids got a big kick out of it and we were on our way.

    Later, the next day, I received a phone call from, of all people, the gas & electric man. He wanted to know when the next nudist meet was and he wanted to buy tickets!! I told him I was only joking, that there was no swim meet. He responded, "you weren't joking, and if you'll get me four tickets I'll make sure you don't get charged for any work I do out there!!" Again, I told him there is no meet and I was only kidding. He refused to believe me, and asked if I would give him the phone number of the Maryland Nudist Society!!

To get him off my back I gave him the phone number of Henry Ciccarone, the Johns Hopkins lacrosse coach. I'm willing to bet, over the years, he made a number of trips to that area, and probably with Chic!!

"GIVE ME AN A!!"

SUBMITTED BY
CARL RUNK

I can't begin to say how excited I was in my first year of coaching. This was the world that I wanted and I wanted to be the best I could. I was assigned as an assistant coach in football at Amphitheater high school and took tremendous pride in my responsibilities. I totally admired the older coaches on the team and listened to every comment they made. These were gentlemen who had played for the University of Arizona and they knew the game. One thing I learned was when we played opponents that were also coached by Arizona alumni, the intensity during the week went up to the next level. We worked extra hard and this was a "must win" situation.

We were playing a cross town rival in a night contest. This was a team that was coached by a very good friend of my mentors. It was an outstanding contest which we won in the last quarter. The coaches were exuberant about the result of the game and we celebrated late into the night. It was decided that we would go over to the home of the opposing coach and tease him a little. When we arrived at his house our whole group stood outside on his front lawn and chanted "Give me an A, give me M, give me P, give me an H, give me an I …..What do you have?" and with a loud chant we yelled "AMPHI!!

When we finished, the lights on the second floor came on and the two windows opened with the opposing coach in one and his wife in the other. It was at that time he started his chant. "Give me an F", and his wife shouted "F". "Give me a U" and she gave him a "U"! Well, it didn't take long to figure out where this was going! "What do you have?!!" They both yelled out what was spelled, shut the windows, turned out the lights and went to bed. Some people just don't have a sense of humor! I was totally embarrassed and decided that I wasn't going to tease any coaches in the future. Some coaches really take losses more seriously than others!!

DICK EDELL'S BIG ESCAPE

SUBMITTED BY
CARL RUNK

My good friend Dick Edell was never known to try to impress or "bull crap" people. He was just a "down to earth" type individual. What you saw was what you got with Rich. One thing for sure ….. if he read you as one of the above, he was soon to depart. He was never one to get involved with coaching clinics as far as I know. If he were asked to speak at a clinic or convention he was reluctant to hold the stage by himself for any period of time before turning the platform over to one of his assistants. And the last place he wanted to be was at a coaches meeting.

We were at the national convention some years ago which was being held in Hoboken, New Jersey. One of the mandatory functions of the convention was the coach's business meeting. This meeting was/and is highly important because of its involvement with each college or university's position on any new rules and/or regulations. All coaches are required to attend the meeting with the results & attendance form being forwarded to each coach's school administration.

Along The Way

It definitely would not be in the coach's best interest if he did not attend this meeting. He would probably hear more than a lecture from his superior when he returned to his office.

The business meeting was well under way for some time when Dick Edell walked into the meeting and just made the "roll call." I was seated in the back when he came in and I laughed like hell at the big "bugger"! Edell's about 6'4" and he's trying to be unnoticeable. He's wearing a wrinkled tan rain over-coat looking like he was involved in a "Sergeant Columbo" look alike contest. The rain coat appeared like it was kept in the glove compartment of his car! As he walked over to me I leaned back and stated "you're really playing it close, Rich!" He whispered to me how he hated these meetings and couldn't wait to get out! He then took an end seat on the right side of the room. I knew exactly what he was up to. He wanted to make an appearance so all in attendance knew he was there and then, when no one was aware, he would quickly slip away leaving all of us to endure the remainder of the meeting.

With the podium and screen on the far left side of the room, everything seemed to be in his favor for the "quick and unnoticed" departure. Why not!!? He was on the role sheet already and everybody saw him there. This was going to be easy!! As the president of the association, standing at the podium, asked that the lights be lowered and all members observe the diagram on the screen, big Rich saw his chance to sneak out. With every one staring at the screen to the right, he quietly rose and started to make a dash for the rear door!! Unfortunately, his cheap "Columbo" jacket got caught in a 6 foot tree plant seated on a table on that side of the room. The sound of that tree crashing to the floor shocked the hell out of everyone in the room. As the lights immediately came on, there stood my big red-faced buddy with that goofy smile on his face, trying to get his jacket unhooked from the tree while trying to replace the tree to its rightful place. It looked like a scene out of a "Laurel and Hardy" movie. To say the least, our buddy was quite

embarrassed and was quite content on staying the rest of the meeting. You had to be there!!! I often wondered if he still has that old jacket? Knowing
him, he probably does!!

THE "LEFT HANDED FACE-OFF"

SUBMITTED BY
CARL RUNK

For many years the right handed face off was a technique taken for granted. Any time the face off was required, after a score, start of the quarter, etc., the players would automatically line up in the center of the field, with the scoring team's face-off man positioning himself first in a face-off position followed by the opposing team's player. At that time the official would check to see that all was proper and then he would blow the whistle to start play.

The hand position on the stick was always with the right hand in the neck position on the stick and the left hand placed at the bottom of the stick. This was the procedure, the way it always was, the protocol of the face-off. The players would, without question, line up and face-off in this manner.

We were at practice the day before a contest when one of our players came to me and said he wanted to face-off but he was at a disadvantage. When I asked him why he simply said he was left handed and this was an advantage for the opposition. He wanted to know why he could not face off left handed, with his dominate left hand at the neck of the stick and his right hand at the bottom of the stick. I told him this is the way it has always been, and that's the rule. He then told me there was not one thing in the rule book stating whether a face-off player could go right handed or left handed. And would you believe, after checking the rule book, he was correct!! There was no mention what's so ever about positioning. Being a person who always takes advantage of a crisis and not let it go to waste, I told the youngster how we would employ the left handed strategy in the contest the next day, which we did. It was midway into the third quarter when we tested the waters for confusion. After we had scored, I had the left handed player go to the face-off area and get down in position, in a left handed manner. The opposing player was totally confused and complained to the official. The official, Mitch Tullai, who was the best in the game, had to study the situation and then he told our youngster he needed to switch his position. It was at that time I asked Mitch why, that there is nothing in the book regarding face-off positioning. He asked that we accept the presently used face-off technique until they could get clarification on it. I told him I would go along with it but it was a definite disadvantage to my player, a form of physical discrimination, and I would probably be seeking legal advice. I should have never said that! I was only jackpotting around. I thought he picked up on that. But he didn't ..... He took me seriously!

    When I arrived home that evening my wife greeted me with the phone. It was a call from "Frenchy Julian", the commissioner of US Lacrosse Officials. Frenchy was one of the most celebrated individuals in the game of lacrosse. A highly popular guy who was loved by everyone familiar with the game. "Kile, (His New York way of saying Carl) What the hell are you doing boy!! We're trying to build this game and you're going to tear it apart by suing us!!?" I quickly explained the situation and said I was only

The "left Handed Face-off"

kidding with Mitch. I thought he read me! I said "I could care less how the hell you face-off!" Frenchy said, "Kile, you can't play with Mitch ….. He's a very serious person!! I'll give him a call and tell him you were only kidding. I'm also going to send a memo out to the association telling them that on the face-off the left hand must always be on the bottom of the stick! "Now, Kile,… I don't want to hear any more bull-s---t from you. You and that damn "Emmer kid" are going to drive me crazy!!"

Frenchy Julian was one of a kind. A Hall of Famer, a lacrosse advocate, and a great friend.

Note: The "Emmer kid" Frenchy was referring to was Jack Emmer, highly successful and outstanding college lacrosse coach and Hall of Fame member.

DRINKING THE WRONG BEVERAGES

SUBMITTED BY
MARK WILLIAMS, TOWSON UNIVERSITY '84

It was 1980 and we had just lost at NC State 18 to 12. This was my 1st year on varsity and on the way home the team was enjoying some adult beverages which I thought was on a "don't ask don't tell" basis judging from the older players. I think Terry Obrien, the trainer, thought it was odd that I asked for a bag of ice for the ride home for a bruise since I did not even play. But nobody likes a warm drink. Well Coach Runk was not very happy about the game or what took place on the bus ride home and let us know it in no uncertain terms at the next practice. Coach told us that we knew who was involved and we should come give him a personal apology. All 170 pounds of me was scared to death. I was one of the last players to make the walk up to coach's office to offer my apology. I walk into coach's office with him sitting behind the desk and started to offer my apology. He looked up from his desk to see me and start laughing. All I could think is that he was playing with my mind and wanted me to relax before he hit this little pencil neck. Coach interrupted me and asked "Who the hell else is going to come in next to apologize, the bus driver?" I was not really sure what he meant but said I was sorry for what happened and got out of there as fast as I could looking over my shoulder the entire length of the hall.

Editors Note: I really didn't think the drinking involved so many people! I would strongly suggest, on bus trips, all coaches should sit in the back!!

The other thing I will never forget was also in 1980 when I got my 1st start against Hofstra on Long Island. I was so nervous I could not even talk without my voice cracking. I overcame my nerves to have a good game in the goal and come within 2 saves of tying the school record for most saves in a game. I was feeling pretty good about my performance and was coming home to play in front of the home town against Hopkins and got the nod to start. This would be a big night to prove that I should be the starter. It was also a big night because it was the first night game in Hopkins history but the only problem was Hopkins did not have lights. They had police trucks parked along the sidelines with lights on top trying to light the field. I might have lasted a little over a quarter before I was pulled from the game. Coach Ardolino came to me at a time out an asked if I could see the ball? He had to know the answer or wanted to see if I was drunk because I was not moving at all. Except maybe when I jumped after the cannon would go off behind me after the goal was scored. I told coach that I could not see it and spent the rest of the game on the bench wondering if I should have lied. That ended the year and my time for feeling good about myself. I was now embarrassed and did not want to use an excuse of not seeing in the dark. I had also summer to think about this and try to improve if for no other reason than to get some of my ego back. It was a very good character builder.

The last story takes me back to NC State again. It was a day game and there were no excuses about not seeing the ball. All I can say is it was a very offensive game. I believe it is still a NCAA record for most goals in a game. The final score was 29 to 19. I think I lasted until the start of the second half at which time coach put Gavin Moag in goal. After about a quarter coach went with Keith Runk. Late in the game I was very surprised when coach turned to me and said get ready to go back in. We could not stop them and they did not do such a good job in stopping us. Another long 6 hour bus ride home just to hear my father ask "what was the score? The TV must have had it messed up because they said something like 29 to 19." I had to inform him that the TV was correct and I made the NCAA record books. Another character builder.

I built a lot of character at TSU.

WHEN THE TWINS WERE BORN

SUBMITTED BY
CARL RUNK

What an exciting time it was in my life when my first children, the twins, were born in Phoenix, Arizona. I was a very proud parent when I first went to the hospital to visit my wife, Joan, and the new arrivals. A procedure used by the hospital nursery attendants, at that time, was to present the new parents with a large instructional record for their use to assist them in their early duties as a parent. At the end of my visit Joan gave me the record and told me to take it home now so we wouldn't need to cart it at the time she and the boys were being released from the hospital. She also told me to stop by the business office on the first floor to sign some papers. After I bid her and the boys good-by for that time, I proceeded to get on the elevator. When I stepped on the elevator there were a number of people also going down. A person of interest was an elderly woman in a wheel chair being attended to by a young lady. As I stood in the elevator staring straight ahead, which people do when they are on an elevator, the woman in the wheel chair, must have seen the record I was carrying and, in an exciting voice, said "Oh my gosh, look what we have here. We have a brand new father. Did you have a boy or a girl, young man?" I responded that I had twin boys. "What a blessing. You must be so proud and happy!!" I'm not sure why I said the following but I did!! I responded, "Not really." To which the elderly woman said "You have twin boys and you're not happy? " Why", she asked. It was at that instant that the elevator door opened. You couldn't have asked for better timing! As I started to walk off the elevator, I responded in a soft voice, "We're not married!! You could have heard a pin drop as I stepped off! This was also at a time when it was heavily frowned on to start a family and not be married! I walked over to the business counter and the attendant asked me why I was laughing. I told her she would never believe what just happened. It was at that time she noticed my record and said, "Oh, we have a new parent! What did you have? At that immediate time, I thought to myself, "Oh man!!, Not again!!"

THE POWER OF THE ASPIRIN

SUBMITTED BY
CARL RUNK

Quite often, as a coach, you are asked to be responsible for many duties, medical training being one. Such was the case for me as lacrosse coach at the University of Arizona. I was very fortunate, since we had no budget for taping, to rely on my friends in the trainers' room, at the University. They would always come through for me with the assistance needed for any injuries on the team.

As a coach, you want to help your kids the best that you can. Your also the first to detect when some of these little pencil-neck ding-a-lings want special attention. They enjoy being stroked and being special. They also place a tremendous amount of confidence in your ability and experience in treating injuries as can be attested in the following situation.

A young outstanding player came to practice in his regular clothes. When I inquired about his not being in his practice gear his response was he had a sore quad-muscle and thought it would be best if he sat out the practice. I assured him that his injury was not all that serious, that I had seen it so many times in football and we could take care of it in just a short period of time with a method I had learned. I then proceeded to ask him where on his thigh was the pain. He showed me and I told him to hold his finger on the exact area until I got the tape. I then took an aspirin, placed it on the designated area, secured it with two pieces of tape looking like an enlarged 4 inch "plus" sign and told the player he should be ready to go in a short period of time. "Let's let the aspirin take effect!'

Would you believe in just a short period of time he came to me and exclaimed he couldn't believe it, that there was no longer any pain in the thigh area and he was ready to go!! The funny thing is the other players wanted the same treatment for their aches and pains. There for a while I felt like an aspirin distributor.

Later, when I told the trainers about my experience with the medical treatments and the teams' reaction, we all got a big laugh out of it.

So much for medical miracles

SOMETIMES YOU GET THE BEAR

SUBMITTED BY
CARL RUNK

A fantastic benefit of coaching is the occasional personal contact a coach receives from former players. I can't begin to tell you what a great feeling it is to hear from young men you have been associated with in earlier years.

I recently received an e-mail from a former player that I haven't seen or heard from in over 48 years. What a pleasant surprise to hear from this individual. His name is Mike St. Ores and he played for me in Arizona. In his email to me, Mike told me exactly what had taken place since our time together. I learned about his vocation, his family, and what he was doing at this time. It was a pleasure to hear how well he was doing. We corresponded for some time through e-mail.

Mike asked me if I could answer a question about a situation that took place in Tucson. Rumor has it there was a carnival at a shopping center with all kinds of rides and entertainment. One of the entertainment areas was a crowd pleaser. There was an animal trainer with a bear.

Along The Way

They were advertising a $100 reward for any person who could wrestle the bear and put him on his back for 3 seconds. Mike told me that many of his teammates profess that "Coach Runk wrestled the hell out of that bear and won the $100!!" He then asked me if this was true or fiction.

Truth or Fiction-

I remember the incident with the bear very vividly. I went up to the carnival a day before to watch how it was run. (I was scouting the bear!!) A young man was trying to wrestle the bear at the time and not doing too well. I thought to myself "I could handle that bugger!" He wasn't that big and didn't seem to be too good on his feet. But as the match went on and the bear was down on his side, the trainer would hit him with a 24 inch long electrical prodder, carrying about 120 volts, in the gonad area. It was like an electrical pep talk! That bears eyes would bulge out, (wouldn't yours?!!) He would let out a roar and I don't think you could hold him down with a Sherman Tank!! It's not the nicest thing to have 120v shoved up your tail!!! With my luck the trainer probably would have misdirected the prod and hit me!! It's really strange what a shot of electricity can do for you!!

I did go there with my kids on a Friday night just to enjoy myself and unfortunately there was a crowd of players there and when they saw me they started chanting "WE WANT RUNK, WE WANT RUNK!!" The trainer even started to yell "Where the hell is Runk?!! Runk … Get up here!!!" I was so embarrassed that I took off for my car, with my kids screaming. They wanted to see the bear. Screw the bear! … I just wanted to get the hell out of there.

I told Mike that's the truth, however, if he wanted to keep the confession to himself and let the rumor continue and grow, I wouldn't mind. Not too many people can be remembered to have wrestled a bear!

A BLUE JAY ALL THE WAY

SUBMITTED BY
BOBBY SCOTT - FORMER JOHNS HOPKINS COACH/ATHLETIC DIRECTOR - LACROSSE HALL OF FAME - A LEGEND IN LACROSSE

In the spring of 1945 I was a ninth grader at Garrison Junior High School when I was asked to join a group of boys to play lacrosse. Our team was called the Forest Park Cubs because Garrison was located just a few blocks from Forest Park High School where most of us would be going the following year.

At the first meeting of our team our coach asked if anyone wanted to be a goal-keeper. Since no one responded, I volunteered to be our goalie. We had played little league baseball in my neighborhood and I had never even picked up a lacrosse stick before. Therefore, it didn't make any difference to me as to where I would play. I was given a stick, a helmet and a pair of gloves, but was told I needed to get a protector. Rather than going downtown to Bachrach-Rasin

Sporting Goods Co. to buy a chest protector, I decided to save money and make my own. I went to our school's cafeteria and confiscated a wooden chair. I punched out the round seat of the chair and took it home. With an ice pick I punched two holes in the seat. I, then, tied a piece of heavy string through the holes so the round wooden seat would be hung around my neck and into position to protect my chest. Under my jersey it wasn't too obvious that I was using such an unorthodox chest protector. I used it the entire season and often surprised our opponent when the ball would come off my "chair-seat" chest protector with a thud!!

Early in that first season of lacrosse, my father drove a group of us players over to Rogers Avenue to watch the forest part varsity team play St. Paul's School. There was a steady rain throughout the game but it didn't slow down Coach Howdy Myers' players from running up a score of 30 to 0! Needless to say, I was really mad at that outcome, and throughout the rest of the 1945 season I checked the Baltimore Sun Paper every day hoping to find St. Paul's on the losing end of a lacrosse game. However, that didn't happen as St. Paul's won every game that season and again in the '46 season.

In the fall of 1946 Howdy Myers left St. Paul's to take the job as head football and lacrosse coach at Johns Hopkins University. Howdy took a number of his star lacrosse players with him to Hopkins. Therefore, as I had hated Howdy and his players when they were at St. Paul's, I continued to do so when they were at Hopkins during the '47 season and even during the spring of my senior year at Forest Park in 1948.

However, there was a complete turnaround of my feelings late in my senior year. Since I had been a second team All Maryland goalie, Howdy called and asked me to come to Hopkins to play lacrosse for him. Needless to say, I was shocked because Howdy and his boys were always for me, "the enemy"! However, since no other college had contacted me, I ended up going to Hopkins in the fall of 1948.

A Blue Jay All The Way

With the freshman rule in effect, I didn't get to play for Howdy until the varsity football season of my sophomore year. I didn't get to play lacrosse for Howdy because he left Hopkins in January of '50 to go to Hofstra University in Long Island, New York. Having been switched from goal to the midfield position during my freshman year, I was fortunate, as a sophomore, to run with the second midfield on the 1950 National Championship team. Quite a thrill for a skinny kid from Forest Park! I continued to play both football and lacrosse at Hopkins, graduating in 1952.

After serving for two years in the Ranger Department of the U.S. Army, I returned to Hopkins in the fall of 1954 as the head coach of the varsity lacrosse team. I was twenty four years old at the time and had no experience whatsoever as a lacrosse coach. That hiring, without question, would never take place in the lacrosse world of today. I proceeded to coach the lacrosse team for twenty years. I was then named director of athletics and served in that capacity for twenty one years.

How ironic was it that I went from a high school lacrosse player who hated the Hopkins lacrosse coach and his teams to spending forty five wonderful years at the university as student, lacrosse coach, and director of athletics.

ALWAYS CHECK YOUR EQUIPMENT

SUBMITTED BY
GENE CORRIGAN FORMER VIRGINIA COACH, NOTRE DAME ATHLETIC DIRECTOR, NCAA PRESIDENT, LACROSSE HALL OF FAME MEMBER

When I think back to my playing days - I go back to Duke in the late 1940's. We had some terrific players who were real characters....Charlie Gilfillen, Brookie Cottman, Rod Boyce and Danny . Our coach was Jack Persons - a man who had never seen lacrosse until he agreed to coach it - but maybe the nicest man any of us ever knew. I think the athletic department only gave him enough money to have on hand about a dozen lacrosse balls - so about 25 percent of our practice time was spent looking for balls. We had more injuries from bee stings and poison ivy than we did from playing lacrosse. He was constantly telling us to take care of our equipment - like checking the screws in our helmets that kept the face mask on. In a game at West Point Brooke Cottman was thrown a long sucker-pass - which arrived at the same time as a West Point defenseman. There on the turf lay Brooke - out cold - and his helmet all over the place. Coach Persons first words...."how many times have I told you to tighten the screws on your helmet"! I don't recall how the game turned out - but none of us ever forgot this scene!

CAN YOU HEAR ME IN THE BACK

SUBMITTED BY
CARL RUNK

For many years I was the master of ceremonies at the National Lacrosse Conventions which included introducing all speakers and clinicians throughout the weekend. At this capacity my responsibilities, along with the introductions, were to make sure all the needs of the speakers were met. This could involve anything from setting up the projectors to preparing the sound system. I was usually fortunate because of the service support that was available. Often I wondered what would be the reaction if there was an interruption in the sound system. Wouldn't it be funny to talk into the microphone in a broken up manner asking "Can you hear me in the back??" and have someone in the rear call out "Can't hear you! ….. You're breaking up!!" I've always thought that would be funny as hell and decided I was going to try it. The first thing to do was to break the sentence down:

"En ou ear me in a ack?"

I tried it at a coaches banquet and really had a lot of fun with it. Some coaches in the back called out they were having trouble hearing me. "You're breaking up!!" But I found it was really effective when I M.C.'d a banquet for about 250 senior citizens down in Florida. The grouchy old buggers started yelling in the back, with some grabbing their hearing aids, checking them out, and others holding their hands up in the air in frustration.

I visited my friend, Dick Edell, when he was in the hospital and shared this story with him. He laughed so hard I was really worried about him hurting himself. He made me tell the story to his wife, Delores, and he enjoyed it more this time than the first. If you were a comedian, you could be very successful if you had a handful of Dick Edells in the audience. He has a fantastic sense of humor.

SUMMER CAMP MANAGER OF THE YEAR

SUBMITTED BY
CARL RUNK

My good friend Sid Jamieson, of Bucknell College, reminded me that the following story must be added in the book. Let us know what you think.

Though we worked extremely hard at our Top Star Camp, we would occasionally like to have some fun with the kids. Midway through camp, at our afternoon camp meeting, I would tell the youngsters we have a special letter we would like them to know about. The letter involves Uncle Leo and his accomplishment. I would also state that Uncle Leo is too modest to read the letter therefore I will read it to the camp. After reading the letter to a standing, screaming ovation for Uncle Leo , with the kids chanting & yelling "UNCLE LEO – UNCLE LEO"!!, I would present him with a gold medal ribbon that I would bring up to camp from school. It was an old conference lacrosse medal that was now being put to good use. It was always difficult to get the ribbon over his big fat head! Many of the kids and visiting parents, taking this presentation very

Along The Way

serious, were overwhelmed, with tears in their eyes, fighting their way to the front to personally congratulate and take pictures with Leo. We would conclude the ceremony with the viewing of three flags, two american and one polish, while being led by "Uncle Leo" in the singing of "God Bless America"!!

Talk about something that could bring a bunch of kids together!!

The following letter is a copy of the letter I would present at camp to Uncle Leo, our camp manager, in front of the campers.

To: *Leo Wisniewski*
      Camp Manager
      Top Star Lacrosse Camp

Dear "Uncle Leo",

Each year it is the responsibility of the "Camps of America" awards committee to select an individual who, through his efforts and initiative, contributes to the positive fitness, growth and behavior of young men in athletics.

It is with great pleasure that I present this year's award, "Camp Manager of the Year", to you, Uncle Leo" on behalf the National Department of Fitness. We are sorry that you are unable to be with us at the ceremonies and we fully understand your wish to be with "your boys" at the Top Star Lacrosse Camp.

Congratulations again, and our appreciation for all you do. Our best to you in the future. May God bless you and may God bless America!

Sincerely yours,

Dan Quale
Vice-President, USA

We did this as a joke but the kids and parents were more gullible than we thought. It was our decision to stop the "Uncle Leo Award". Too serious!! They, (the kids and parents) took the fun out of it, and we also had the vice-presidents' son at camp!!

THE TAIL GATERS

SUBMITTED BY
CARL RUNK

One of the negative experiences I found difficult to accept, late in my tenure as a coach, was the parent involvement and tail-gating. I was never one to participate in, or enjoy, tail-gating! I always felt it opened up an opportunity for parents to vent their emotions toward the coach. "You're not playing my son!" ... "You should've switched the goalie earlier!" .... "Could've won the game if you'd run the zone!" are just typical comments a coach might hear at these times. I remember, at away games, telling the players and parents "You can tail-gate for ½ hour. When the bus horn sounds, we're leaving!" Most of the time the parents wanted to make it a three hour affair! I just wanted to get out of there .... Especially after a loss!! I would sit on the bus and read anything available. And I refused to go out and mingle with the group. Now my coaching staff was not as strong as I was. As soon as the scent of the barbecued beef, hamburgers, hotdogs & chicken wings hit them .... they were gone!! And what really upset me was they never brought anything back for the "Old Man!!"

They could've said "Hey Coach, gotcha a nice barbecue sandwich and a few wings!"

No Way!! And since I would sit in the front of the bus I really believe some of the parents, whose sons didn't see the playing time they thought they deserved, would get back at me by setting up the grill and table right in front of the bus so I would get full view of what was available to eat and drink. Just didn't seem fair, but "you make your bed … you sleep in it!!" However, they really didn't know how close they came to breaking me down!

Do you think I'm a little paranoid?!!

PARENTS WITH AN ANSWER

SUBMITTED BY
CARL RUNK

After I left Towson University I was contacted by a local high school, Hereford High, asking if I could possibly coach the lacrosse team. Since I would run at the school during the day and it was only a mile from my home, I thought it was a good idea and accepted. And I must say, the faculty of the athletic department was just an outstanding group of coaches. These were dedicated young men whom you would be proud to have coached your child! At the helm of the group was Mike Kalusz, the athletic director. I see nothing but a positive future for Mike in the profession of education. He was a very fair, congenial, and compassionate person, highly respected by his staff. Any time there was any kind of a problem, Mike would try to nip it at the bud. There were times when he would confront you as a coach, not because he wanted to, but because the low pain tolerant principle would want an answer. I recall having a tremendous week-end with our team winning the Maryland State Lacrosse Championship. That following Monday I was talking to my defensive coach, Steve Turnbaugh, also an excellent football coach but more importantly, an outstanding coach of young men, when Mike passed by and asked me to stop by his office when I get a chance. As I came into Mike's office he asked me to close the door. I immediately burst into laughter. I said "Mike, I've learned a long time ago that any time an administrator calls you in his office and tells you to close the door, you're in trouble! Let's hear it, buddy. What did I do wrong?!!" Trying to be as pleasant as possible, Mike told me "some parent has filed a complaint with the principle and he, the principle, wants me to confront you!" I asked Mike "did I punch the kid?" He said no. I asked "Did I grab him by the face-mask and shake him up a little?" He, again, said no. "Did I swear in front of him, using the Lord's name in vain or the "F" word?" Again, his answer was no! "Did I belittle or humiliate him verbally in front of the team?" "No" was his answer. As I was running out of "Did I's", I finally asked, "Did I fondle the kid?!! He laughed and said no. As I proceeded to sit down in the chair I said "Mike, I've covered all my bases, you aint got a leg to stand on!!" "What the hell is the complaint?!" He replied, "Coach, the parents feel their son should have played more and you didn't give him the opportunity to progress like the other boys!" Mike was really embarrassed to have to call me in about this situation. He told me it was something the principle and he should be addressing, not the coach. I told him I appreciated his honesty and concern for me. The boy in question was a sophomore at the time and I can truthfully say that during his future tenure as a player, anytime I was confronted by his phony parents coming over to talk about the game or anything, my response was short, very short and complemented with a cold walk-away!!! Screw the parents and the boat they came in on!!

SIMILAR SITUATION – DIFFERENT PARENTS

SUBMITTED BY
CARL RUNK

In my final year at Hereford High School, I was fortunate to have an outstanding young group of players. We were very successful on the field, going undefeated and winning the state championship. However, near the end of the season, before the state tournament, I was contacted by Mike Kalusz, the athletic director for a conference. Evidently, one of the parents was livid that his son was not seeing the playing time they, the parents, thought he should see. He should be in the game more. The parent sent an email to the principle of the school demanding that I be made aware of his feelings and that I meet with him, face to face, to explain why his son was being mishandled this way. I told Mike I looked forward to meeting with this parent, face to face, any time he was available. Mike offered to have one of the full time coaches attend the meeting also but I informed him there was no need. Been there ... done that ... many times in my coaching tenure!

Along The Way

As I sat in Steve Turnbaugh's football office to meet the parent, there was a knock on the door. I requested that he come in, the door was open. From the way the email read, I expected a large, boisterous person to come barging in. To my surprise, it was just the opposite. The parent was small and thin, with a very soft voice. "Hi Coach Runk. How are you today?" Like he gave a damn!! Very business-like, I responded, "How can I help you?" Then it started. "My son has been playing lacrosse since he was five years old. When he played in the juniors leagues, they won the championship. When he played summer league, he played with the best players in the league and was a star. On the junior varsity team he ran first midfield and the team won the junior varsity championship. Now that he is a member of the varsity team, he's not seeing much playing time. There has got to be a reason as to why he's not playing. Can you tell me why??"

<u>Note</u> - At this specific time it is important that the reader be aware of the following. I have always been an advocate of recording player evaluation drills in lacrosse. These drills would include velocity shooting drills, both running and standing still, agility stick drills showing stick handling abilities, and scoop & shoot drills. All drills included both the right and left hand. These were informative drills that players participated in which would show both strengths & weaknesses of individual players. In essence, telling the players were there was improvement needed. The player knew exactly where he stood compared to his teammates.

In a very diplomatic and compassionate manner, I explained the difference between the jv and the varsity. I mentioned there is a big difference physically between the jv and the varsity. On the jv's, the youngsters are basically going through puberty, that they are physically in changing times. On the varsity, the players have passed that stage, have hair on their legs and are more adult. "Your son hasn't reached that stage yet." But in time, he'll mature and hopefully improve." I thought that answer would calm his

Similar Situation – Different Parents

feelings somewhat but to no avail. His response was "But how come he is not playing?!!" Again, I tried to diplomatically explain that many of the youngsters are ahead of his son, at this time, because they are physically stronger. He should see a big change with some sort of participation in a weight program.

In a demanding manner he asked , "That boy should be playing! How come he is not playing?!" It was at this point of the meeting that all the diplomacy I had tried to involve in our discussion was severely depleted! This parent was forcing me to eliminate courtesy and tell him just why his son was not participating. And it was a road I did not want to travel. "Our goal in this program is to give every player the opportunity to advance in the skills that will contribute to the success of the program. We are not, however, an equal opportunity agency and have, as a philosophy, the desire to win the state championship! Regarding your son: Our evaluation tests indicate he scores well below average in agility, speed, quickness, and stick skills. At the present time his shot velocity falls below the norm. His ability to handle the lacrosse stick with his non-dominate side is practically non-existent. I'm sorry to have to tell you this!" I was literally shocked to hear the parent's response to my player appraisal.

"Yeah, but how come he's not playing?!!" What didn't he understand about my explanation?!! Where did I go wrong in my presentation? I couldn't believe it! Sometimes they only hear what they want to hear. And so much for evaluation drills!! Quite often it's difficult for a male parent to accept the fact that what has been produced by his loins is not always perfect.

Note: I've often wondered how successful that youngster would have been if he'd gone out for the golf or rifle team. Guess we'll never know.

THE HOSPITALIZATION OF DICK EDELL

SUBMITTED BY
PAUL GRIFFIN SENIOR ASSOCIATE DIRECTOR OF ATHLETICS GEORGIA TECH ATHLETIC ASSOCIATION

One of my favorite lacrosse coach colleagues has been Dick Edell. Our sideline confrontations have been exciting, challenging, competitive and more one-sided than I would have liked. Since his departure from the University of Baltimore and my exit from lacrosse coaching, we have remained close friends; a relationship that I hope prospers well into the future.

In the context of today's world of college lacrosse, it seems odd that in the 1970's the head coach of a Division II program wore many hats from sports medicine, equipment manager, and field maintenance. At Roanoke College, our practice and playing field (one in the same) was experiencing some significant drainage challenges and as such we could not maintain a good surface as we transitioned from the cold of winter into the beautiful spectacle of spring.

Approximately five miles from campus was a sprawling facility which housed a Veteran's hospital, rehabilitation facility, and housing for disabled veterans. The facility had to encompass 500+ acres and was quite the scenic enclave.

Somehow I decided to convince the VA to allow the Roanoke lacrosse team to use part of its pasture land that fronted the highway as our practice field and game facility. The space was bordered by some hills and berms so a natural stadium bowl was easy to establish. We mowed the field, staked the game lines, and lined what emerged as RC Lax Stadium.

I then convinced the Roanoke Athletic Director to allow us to purchase an Army surplus transport bus to carry our team from campus to the VA on a daily basis. The bus was driven by our face-off specialist which is a separate set of stories (tales) that are incredible.

On a beautiful April Saturday afternoon, two nationally ranked teams faced off at the RC Lax Stadium, aka the VA Hospital. The University of Baltimore and Roanoke College were both positioning their teams for a post season berth as in those days the DII and DIII teams were combined in one NCAA tournament. It was an odd mix of scholarship programs and non-scholarship schools.

The game was hotly contested throughout and during the second half; we (Roanoke College) began to pull away from the BU squad coached by Dick Edell. Because it was such a pretty spring afternoon, the field was ringed with fans outfitted with blankets, coolers, and all of the essentials. The clamor also attracted several of the VA patients and the game served as a magnet for the patients' afternoon recreation.

Dick called timeouts late in the third quarter and early in the fourth. As I glanced down the sideline at my colleague's bench, I noticed that three VA patients had found their way to the BU bench and were enjoying sitting on the bench and drinking the Gatorade. In the second timeout, the VA patients decided to join the BU huddle and eavesdrop on Coach Edell's strategic discussion with his team. It all seemed rather bizarre.

Roanoke College prevailed on this day and following the game, Dick Edell was interviewed by the Roanoke Times and was asked "when did you sense that Roanoke had the game well in hand". As only my good friend could express, Dick responded "I realized that Paul had gone to all lengths to secure victory during a time out when the best strategic suggestions were provided by three hospital patients Paul had placed on our bench. I asked one of the patients if I could get one of those plastic wrist bands and check in to the facility in time to have dinner as the rest of the day was not going very well."

Needless to say, the BU squad did not dine with the VA patients that day although it may have been better than the fare enjoyed on the long bus ride back to Baltimore. To this day, Dick and I tease each other about how crazy this scene was and how the game has changed so much since then.

WHAT STRANGE CREATURES THESE COACHES ARE

SUBMITTED BY
CARL RUNK

Years back I was involved a situation that was quite odd. Sometimes, as coaches, we get a little carried away and literally do the strangest things. It could be wearing a certain tie to a ball game because in the last contest we were wearing that same tie when we won and felt it would be unlucky to change. It could even be not changing the underwear. Maybe it was using the same bus driver for all away games. Any number of things fit the circumstances. I was in a position where a certain coach irritated the hell out of me because of something he did, and I refused to communicate with that individual for over two years.

I made sure we never had words at clinics or lacrosse functions. Anytime our teams would compete, I would never stand in the center of the field, prior to the game, to exchange discussion or words. I always took a stand at the end line on my side of the field. After the game I refused to get in line and shake hands. I always found something else to keep me occupied. One day I received a note in the mail from this particular coach and it was a very humble expression of respect and friendship. He said he was not aware of what he did that bothered me but if he had hurt me in some way, he was truly sorry. He wanted us to be on a friendly basis. I was really touched by that letter and I began to think to myself .... "What was it he said or did that made me so upset?" And do you know, for the life of me, I couldn't remember! I then thought how could I not speak to a person if I didn't know why I stopped talking to him in the first place. It just didn't seem to be the proper thing to do. After my soul searching period, I got on the phone and called the coach, telling him I was touched by his note, excusing myself for the childish behavior and offered to buy him a drink the next time we met.

Our friendly relationship lasted for about a year, then one day while I was reminiscing, I remembered why I was so p—ssed off with him in the first place.

Would you believe I stopped talking to him again!! Cut him off from any relationship whatsoever! Am I different? Is there something missing here? How would any other coach re-acted to the same situation?

An old polish philosophy: "When you hold a grudge ... hold a grudge!! Go after the jugular!" .... And I'm not even polish!

A COLD WHIRLPOOL

SUBMITTED BY
MATT PALUMB SYRACUSE ALL-AMERICAN ASSISTANT ATHLETIC DIRECTOR FOR DEVELOPMENT SYRACUSE

It's the summer of '93, and I am at Rutgers trying out for the '94 World Team. At the time, I'm nursing a sprained ankle. Prior to one of the tryout sessions, I'm in the training room at Rutgers and have my foot and ankle dunked in the cold whirlpool. I've always been a wuss about the cold and hated cold whirlpools, and this one was the coldest that I'd ever been in. I was by myself in the whirlpool room, and was rocking back and forth on the edge of the tub, and was literally close to making whining noises because of how cold it was. As I looked out of the whirlpool room, I could see the legendary Vinnie Sombrotto walking down the hallway, heading for the cold whirlpool, and on the verge of making his 4th World Team. I had never met Vinnie before, but anybody who had anything to do with lacrosse in those days knew who he was. I was a scrawny 24 year old goalie from upstate NY, and he was at least 10 years older than me, a native Long Islander, had something to do with the Teamsters, and a lacrosse legend. Point being, I certainly didn't want to show Vinnie that I was about in tears because of the whirlpool. Vinnie walks into the whirlpool room, just after I gather myself and put the toughest face on that I could come up with. He nods at me, but doesn't really say anything. He's got the Daily News and The New York Post under his arm. He sits on the opposite side of the tub and, without hesitation, plops his whole leg in the freezing water, foot to his hip. He immediately opens up his paper and starts to read. In typical tough-guy fashion he doesn't flinch, make a face, or react at all. I can barely contain how miserably cold I am and how much my foot hurts. After about 30 seconds, Vinnie looks up from his paper at me and says, "Yo, this ain't chicken soup, huh??" I absolutely started laughing my ass off, as his delivery was beyond classic. I will never forget my first encounter with Vinnie, and have since that time, gotten to know him well and laugh about that story often.

A YOUNG MAN ANY COACH WOULD LOVE TO HAVE

SUBMITTED BY
CARL RUNK

I received the following letter many years ago, had it framed and placed in my office until my retirement.

The young man, (name withheld), was a stone bullcrapper!! He came to Towson as a walk-on and walked off after the first day of fall ball. They tell me he lasted in school a few weeks before leaving. Rumor has it he's employed as a toll gate operator somewhere in New York.

1978   Room 348 West Hall
*   S.U.N.Y. A&TC*
*   Morrisville, NY 13408*

Carl Runk
1518 Winford Road
Baltimore, Md. 21239

Dear Sir:
*   I am attending SUNY at Morrisville A&TC. Having attended for one year as well as playing lacrosse on the varsity level, I feel very confident in reaching my goal in education, M.S., and also in the sport of lacrosse, All American.*
*   Lacrosse is a team sport. I believe in competition. I also believe the better your competitive environment, the faster I'll improve to reach that more excellent stage.*
*   My Motto!! Practice every day! Perfect practice does make perfect. Running to build endurance, exercising for strength, and drills for the power to resist defeat.*
*   Having already read the 1977-78 Towson State University catalog, Mr. Runk, I agree with the University philosophy. An education is indispensable for the preservation of a free society, and let me add, let every man exercise his free will.*
*   Towson State? A better place to excel. I am anticipating a reply from you.*
*   Sincerely yours,*

It's the kind of bull-crap letter every coach has probably received, sometime or other, in his tenure!

FRIENDLY CONSOLING

SUBMITTED BY
CARL RUNK

One of the benefits of having a successful summer camp is getting to know many coaches on a friendly basis. It's a completely relaxed atmosphere and you're able to really enjoy the relationship with the staff.

This was the case of a young coach with whom I became very friendly. For obvious reasons I'll refer to him as Coach Bob. Coach Bob was just starting out in his career as a coach and had a small apartment in the borough of Gettysburg. The majority of coaches at the camp lived in the dormitories on campus and didn't have the conveniences of air conditioning, television or a refrigerator. Bob did!! "Uncle Leo" and I drove him home one night and found that he also had exceptional other conveniences. Bob was living with his girlfriend. He introduced her to us and said they had plans to be married in the future. They seemed to be the perfect couple. One thing for sure ... his sleeping partner was a hell of a lot better than mine at the time. I had to sleep with that grouchy old man whose snoring was just unbearable!! Both Leo and I were very happy for Bob and his wife to be.

Later in the summer in Gettysburg, but with a different camp, "Uncle Leo" and I bumped into Coach Bob at the cafeteria. He was friendly but just not his regular self. He seemed quite despondent, staring into a cup of coffee as if searching for answers. We asked if everything was alright … Was anything wrong? Bob's response was a little surprising. He said he and his girlfriend had broken up right after the first camp. She said she was going to her high school re-union. While there at the re-union, she met an old friend and within two weeks they were married. This was shocking news and we felt we would have to console Bob. Leo, having the ability to be the most compassionate person I have ever known, starts to tell Coach Bob he knows exactly how he feels. After hearing this I'm wondering where the "old man" (Leo) is going with this story. He places his arm around Bob's shoulders in a comforting manner and starts his tale of woe. "Bob, I experienced a similar situation when I was a young man. I was dating a lovely young lady for a long period of time. A very good friend of mine was getting married and I took the beautiful young lady to the wedding. While there at the wedding, I met a female friend that I hadn't seen in a few years, became infatuated with her and ended up leaving my date at the wedding while I ran off with the new relationship. I don't know how my date ever got home but I do know this … the one I took home dropped me like a hot potato!! I knew what I did was wrong and I tried very hard to apologize to the girl I was dating but she would have nothing to do with me. I never heard from or saw her again! And I often wonder about her. What she looks like … Is she married? How's she doing? I guess I really messed up!! So Bob, I kind of know how you feel."

Leo almost had me in tears with this story. It was like one of the soap shows you see on television. He then gets up from the table, pats Coach Bob on the shoulder and walks over to the ice cream machine to get his daily 3 lb. dip of soft ice cream. At this point, I'm not sure what the hell to do. I'm surely not going to tell the distraught

Friendly Consoling

youngster another tear-jerking story like Leo's. In my comforting way, I walked over to Bob, placed my hand on his shoulder and said "Bob, if it will make you feel any better, I saw "Uncle Leo's" ex-girlfriend two weeks ago. She was on the back end of a Harley Davidson, she's got an 18 inch neck and weighs about 250 lbs!! But please don't tell him. It would tear him up!!"

Would you believe I got a great laugh out of Coach Bob.

KIDS SAY THE DARNDEST THINGS

SUBMITTED BY
CARL RUNK

A characteristic you'll see quite often in the city is people will usually sit out front their home after dinner or in the early evening. Our row home was in the city and had a comfortable porch out front. As usual, the neighbors on both sides of my home were sitting out front relaxing. On my left lived an eldely retired Italian couple, Mr. & Mrs. Mano. They were from Italy and spoke broken English. A beautiful two-some. On the right lived a middle age couple whom I referred to as the "Radar" group. The wife's main function was to know exactly what was going on at anytime, 24/7, and report it to who- ever was interested in hearing it. She could always be seen peeking out the window or through the door. This was, for me, irritating at times when it involved me, but interesting when I was being informed about other people.

 I was arriving home from practice on a beautiful spring evening. As was customary, my wife, Joan, would have the kids, the boys, in the bathroom taking a bath before going to bed. As I got out of the car and started up the steps, the boys poked their heads out the window and started to yell in an exciting manner. "Hey Dad, hurry and come up to the bathroom. We want you to see this!! You won't believe it!!! When you pour cold water on your gonads they disappear!!" This was truly something you wouldn't expect eighteen year olds to do! (Only kidding!)

To say the least, this was a totally embarrassing situation. I didn't know which way to turn and couldn't get into the house soon enough! To my surprise, the kids' observation meant nothing to the relaxing neighbors as they just sat there on the porch and greeted me on the way in. There was no reaction from them at all. It didn't take me long to realize that the poor souls didn't understand the meaning of the word "gonads"! I was sparred again!

THE BARBERSHOPPERS

SUBMITTED BY
CARL RUNK

I have always enjoyed participating in the singing of barbershop music. As a young coach in Arizona I was also a member of the SPEBSQA society which is the supporting society for barbershop quartet singing in America. We never turned down an opportunity to sing at community events and city & state functions.

A few years back, there was something I wanted to do at the national lacrosse convention being held in Hoboken, New Jersey. It involved barbershop quartet singing. Since I was the master of ceremonies, along with being on the speaking agenda, this would give me an extraordinary opportunity to attempt this feat. My plan was to contact the local Hoboken SPEBSQA chapter and see if I could recruit a base, baritone, and tenor singers to help me. I was very fortunate that three gentlemen agreed to assist in this ordeal. My connection with them was strictly on the phone where we decided what song(s) we would sing. We met for the first time at the lecture hall just before I was about to speak. I had them strategically placed along the front row in the hall. At a select time, I would look like

I was randomly choosing three coaches to step up to the stage with me. Little did anyone know that the three were pre-chosen.

It worked out great! I ended my lecture by telling the audience (1200 attendees) "there must be harmony in what you're doing ... with everyone on the same note ... It's important that you hit the same blending chord!" It was at that time I said, "Here .... Let me show you ... give me any three coaches out there!" I then proceeded to point to the three singers who were spread out in the front row, inviting them up to the stage with me. Once they were assembled on stage facing the audience, I turned and asked the three "Are you ready?" With that, I got along side of the so-called coaches and we sang a hell of a rendition of "Coney Island Baby". The crowd went berserk!! After finishing the song, one of the singers said "Hey, they really like us! Let's sing another!! I told him "Let's not press our luck and get out of here while we can!! The crowd was ecstatic. It was just a super way to end the evening. I took the barbershoppers up to my room where I had refreshments available and we sang into the early morning hours. They left half potted and were overwhelmed with joy stating that the guys back in the chorus will never believe "we sang in front of 1200 people!!"

THE ANNUAL POLICE DEPARTMENT PICNIC

SUBMITTED BY
CARL RUNK

Many years ago, while teaching in a Tucson, Arizona school district and also coaching lacrosse at the University of Arizona, my family and I were invited to attend a picnic sponsored by the Police Department. As fate would have it, I was awarded a 1st place door prize which I never received. In order to have some fun, I sent a letter to the editor of the local newspaper. The letter was
published shortly afterwards.

2 September 1965

Dear Sir:

Approximately one year ago I was invited to the Tucson City Police Department's annual picnic, which was held in New Tucson. Along with my family, I was overwhelmed and humbly accepted. I find it hard to express the exuberance displayed by my family, especially my four young children who consistently insisted the sun rises and sets on our police department.

To my own enjoyment, I was told Marshall K-Gun, the local TV personality, would be present.

My family has never experienced a more enjoyable and hospitable atmosphere. Along the course of the day it was announced I was the recipient of a 1st place door prize. It was only natural that my respect, as well as the children's admiration, toward the Police Department, increased immensely.

We were to receive an appliance of our choice.

I have often wondered in this past year if our Police Department was pulling my leg, so to speak, as I have never received my prize. They have, however, been very efficient in our personal relationships regarding traffic procedures, and I find it hard to believe they would be negligent in this matter.

Ever so often I receive a call from the individual who was the second place door prize winner. He, too, has been neglected and calls me on the phone, occasionally, seeking comfort and reassurance regarding his belated gift. We are both naturalized citizens and my wife and children are an avid listening audience to the "police calls" on the radio. I hoped, maybe, this might influence their final decision.

This ordeal has put a tremendous mental strain on all involved. My children can't believe that such a situation could exist, my wife has shown a lack of interest in her daily cooking procedures, which is affecting us all, and I don't know how long I can evade the family's persistent inquiries. The second place winner, a member of the Tucson Fire Department, claims he finds it hard to concentrate on his work as his mind repeatedly reverts to this unpleasant situation. I often find myself confronted with this familiar predicament as I will run off to work, completely forgetting to put the kids in the car or take the trash out.

I would appreciate your investigation.
(Name withheld for obvious reasons)

Approximately 3 days after this letter was published, our home was visited by blaring sirens and flashing lights. The congenial officer at the door said it was his duty to deliver the gift, only because he had lost in the vote.` Later in the week, while conversing with friends about this situation, at a University of Arizona football game, I overheard a lady seated behind me, call out to her husband, "Charlie, come over here ….. Here's the nut that sent in that letter to the editor!"

THE SUPER BOWL PARTY

SUBMITTED BY
CARL RUNK

For many years we would celebrate, like many others, the Super Bowl game with a large party at our house. It was a joyous time and involved a large number of people. My wife, Joan, and I would supply the food, beverages, and hospitality for the crowd. We would also give out gifts, that we had collected beforehand, from different places. Most of everything that was given out was donated from beer distributors, liquor distributors and various companies. A special time at the party was when we gave everyone a "Super Bowl at the Runks" T-shirt. (From what I'm hearing now, that t-shirt is going for a lot of money at the auctions.) Each person, on arriving, was given their name tag with a number. At half time, the gifts were shown to the crowd with sounds of "oows & aahs!! Individual numbers, placed in a jar, were selected and if the number corresponded with the number a person was wearing, he/she would win that prize. It was just a great time.

In preparing for the coming super bowl party, my friend Willie asked me about the expense of having the party and was a bit surprised when I mentioned, besides the food, I would get the beer donated. "There's no way!!! You mean to tell me you just call a beer company and tell them you want some beer donated for a party your throwing and they would oblige and send it??!" I assured him that's what I did. He continued to disagree. "Who the hell do you think you are and why should that company send you anything!! I responded "I'm not sure why but they do it and I appreciate it."

Ironically, Willie worked for a beer & liquor distributor company in the Baltimore area. I asked Willie who was his supervisor or administrative leader at that time. He gave me the name of the person and the phone number. Later I called and requested to speak to that person. "Hi Carl, how can I help you?" I said, John, It's that time of year again. We're having our coaches super bowl party and I'm calling you to find out if we can count on you again this year to help us with refreshments. John responded, "Sure, Carl, what will you need? I answered, "About 8 cases, 4 regular and 4 light." John said that would be no problem. He then asked, "How are you going to pick them up?" I answered "Since Willie Metzger works for you and is coming to the party, if you could put them in his car, I'm sure he wouldn't mind delivering them!!"

One of the funniest sights I saw was Willie coming up to the house carting the beer on a two wheel dolly!!

DUFFY

SUMITTED BY
CARL RUNK

As previously stated, the gatherings at the Super Bowl party were extremely entertaining and an event we all looked forward to. Prior to the game in 1983 the following message was sent out to all expected to attend.

January 30, 1983

TO: Invited Guests
FR: The Runks
RE: Super Bowl Request

Coaches,

We would like to take this opportunity to thank you all for being with us on this day of fellowship and fun. Our only hope is that you are satisfied with the results of this year's big game. Last year's super bowl party was, without a doubt, a great afternoon.
Our dog, Duffy, a $500.00 white shepard, a descendant of the "Broumel Von Schlepner" line, whose ancestors were viewed breeding in an alley by Adolph Hitler while reviewing a division of German soldiers in downtown Berlin, unfortunately had a

heart attack at the conclusion of last year's party. Three weeks and $350.00 later, Duffy left us for that canine country in the sky. We were informed by our veterinarian doctor that Duffy was unable to pass ¾ lb. of pepperoni, the size of a baseball, lodged in the lower intestine. This, he said, was a contributing factor in her difficulties.

If per chance you should see any animals or our children wandering around during the party, Joan and I would really appreciate your refraining from feeding them.

Otherwise, have a great time!
Joan & Carl

IF HE GOES TO CAROLINA ... LEAVE HIM!!!

SUBMITTED BY
CARL RUNK JR. TOWSON '84

My name is Carl Runk Jr. and I thought I might include the following story for publication in my father's book.

Years ago our family would spend the summers at Ocean City, Maryland. It was a place where the whole family could work and relax. Since my dad was on a "nine month teaching contract", he had to find work during the summer. Obviously, Ocean City had plenty of possibilities for employment. My mom and dad made sure my brother Keith and I were kept busy at the beach running our beach stands. It was a great way for young kids to grow up. I think I spent more time in the water surfing than I did watching my beach stand. The young gals were more than pleased to watch and rent umbrellas & air mats as long as I bought them lunch! On one particular day while I was surfing on my mat in the ocean I heard screaming and a frantic call for help from a young guy who was isolated and in distress. Evidently, he got caught up in a "rip-tide" and was bobbing up and down, really struggling to survive. No doubt, he was in deep trouble. I started paddling as fast and hard as I could to get to him. When I got there I reached out and grabbed him, pulling him onto the mat. I told him to just hang on and I would get us to calmer waters. After we got to the beach I noticed that the person in distress was a lacrosse playing friend, Tommy Sears. Tommy just graduated from Calvert Hall High School in Baltimore, and was one of the most award winning goalies in high school lacrosse. We both sat on the beach thinking about what we just went through. I asked Tommy, in a kidding way, "Since I just saved you from that "rip-tide" don't you think you should consider playing lacrosse for my dad at Towson?" Tommy replied he was going to North Carolina to play. I told him, while laughing, "I wish I would have known that before I helped you!!

Later in the evening, I told my dad about my experience in the ocean with Tommy. His response was, "You should have asked him, before you pulled him on the mat, where he was going to school. If he tells you North Carolina, leave him out there!!"

KEEPING THE OFFICIALS ON THEIR TOES

SUBMITTED BY
CARL RUNK

We've made tremendous advancement in the game of lacrosse in coaching, perfecting technique, strategy, and officiating. This is mainly because of the research made available by the coaches, lacrosse enthusiasts, and the overwhelming growth of the game. It wasn't always that way. In the '60's & '70's the game was in a transforming mode and had a different complexion. One example would be officiating. Probably the most experienced officials could be found in the Maryland and New York areas, where the game was highly popular. Growth in some of the smaller states, Delaware, New Jersey, Virginia, to name a few, suffered somewhat because of lack of exposure and numbers. Delaware, always a strong opponent, was a contest where I worried quite a bit. It was difficult as hell to play Delaware at their place. Anything could happen, and usually did! In preparing for that contest, I tried to make sure I covered all bases. And this involved prepping the officials. I remember talking with the officials at the pre-game meeting about game procedure and various situations. Once this was over, the officials would ask if I had any other concerns. On this particular day I responded, "Not really, but do you know of any reason Noel Turner is at this game? (Noel Turner was the lacrosse commissioner for the state of Delaware at that time.) "Is he here evaluating or just here to watch a good game?" Obviously, the commissioner wasn't at the game but I just threw that in to shake them up a little, with the hope of keeping them on their toes throughout the entire game. It was funny to see the officials become very alert and start looking into the stands. "Where did you see him?" I told them we talked for a short time when we got off the bus. It was great to see how professional they became with their game mechanics. If you filmed the game, you could use it as the "Proper Technique of a Lacrosse Official, 101" teaching course. I would use this strategy again, at Delaware or other games, as long as the officials were different. We always stressed trying to get the most out of our players and I didn't see anything wrong with trying to do the same with officials.

STILL ON THEIR TOES!

SUBMITTED BY
CARL RUNK

Another lacrosse official strategy I used quite often when traveling to another state: At the end of the pre-game meeting with the officials we would agree on contest rules and the officials would tell me the exact time, according to their watches. I would ask that I set my watch specifically with theirs. And then I would tell them I doubt if we should have any problems with time as I'm really pleased with my watch, …. "It was given to me by the Maryland Lacrosse Officials Organization for outstanding sportsmanship!" Some were gullible enough to accept that statement. Unfortunately, not as many as I wanted.

Always observe road signs

THE NEW VAN

SUBMITTED BY
CARL RUNK

The relationships you develop with your players, support personnel, and all associated within your sport, are life lasting. They are particular and you cherish beautiful memories from a time that seems to quickly slip away. I was very fortunate after my 25th year of coaching at Towson University to be honored by both friends and players, past & present, at a banquet. It was an evening I always will remember and it culminated with the gift of a new luxury van, something my wife and I had dreamed about for a long time.

I remember how excited I was about the van as I drove it around and showed it to all my friends. Just a few days after receiving the gift, I went to a local mall in the Towson area to pick up some supplies at Jim Darcangelo's "LAX WORLD". Jimmie was an ex player of mine and a very prominent businessman.

There were two ways I could approach the "Lax World", store. One was at the front lot which was wide open but you'd have to walk up a number of steps. I wasn't into that, and didn't want to park the van near all those cars owned by "reckless commoners" The more convenient path was the back lot which allowed me to enter from the rear of the building. I chose the more convenient way, the back lot. What I didn't take into account was that the passage way entrance was specifically marked with a warning sign stating "no vehicles over the height of 7'6"!! For some reason I was under the impression I was driving my old pick-up truck. I learned an important lesson that day. There are some things that are quite different between a regular vehicle and a luxury van!

Size is one!! As I came through the passage way I heard a very deep ugly sound and wondered "What the hell was that!!" I stopped the van, got out looked completely around the vehicle and for some unknown reason instantly looked back at the entrance only to see that warning sign which was bigger than hell! The first thought that crossed my mind was, "Oh hell!! I've just created a new sun roof on this thing!!" I was literally sick to my stomach. What a stupid blunder!! Using the ladder on the back of the van, I was able to get to the top and see what kind of damage was created. What a relief to find there was no new sun roof and there was only a wide scratch that could be easily buffed out.

I went into the store and was quickly approached by two salesmen of outstanding popularity, Bobby Scheck and Bobby Martino, both all-american lacrosse players and recent participants of the "Lacrosse World Games". Bobby Scheck had played for me at Towson. "Coach Runk,

The New Van

how are you doing with that new van? When are we going to get a chance to ride in it?!" I told them I had brought the van with me and I also explained my dilemma. Both guys said they were sorry to hear about the predicament and Scheck questioned me regarding how I was going to get off the lot. Damn!! That never crossed my mind. Another major problem!! I asked if they could help me as I was leaving the lot. It was decided to place card board on the roof to be used as a cushion. This would eliminate the rubbing on the roof and I'd be home free. As fate would have it, it was more difficult getting the van out than getting it in. Our next decision was to let the air out of the tires, lowering the vehicle an inch or so and allowing the room needed to get through that damned door way! I also had both guys stand on the rear bumper and watch to see how close we were to the overhang. When we were able to clear the passage way, I told Scheck & Martino that this was a very embarrassing situation and I'd like them to assure me this wouldn't get out to the lacrosse world. There was no need for anyone to know about this. They both agreed and said "Coach, What happened here today will not get out to the public!!" I thanked them for their understanding and also for their help, at which time I drove off with the newly christened van, including four almost flat tires. Fortunately, I was near a gas station where I would stop to attend to the tires. The gas station attendant complemented me on the van but was inquisitive as hell regarding the four flat tires. I didn't know what to tell him so I told him the truth. He also said he would not inform anyone about the story of the van. Finally, later in the morning, I arrived at school. I had all that had happened in the past 45 minutes behind me and I was ready to attack the day! As I opened my office door the first thing to draw my attention was my telephone with all those lights blinking. I hit the button to play the recordings and would you believe the first call was from an ex player calling in from Delaware stating he just got word from another player in Jersey asking if he had heard about what happened to Coach Runk and the new van!!! I am totally convinced that Bobby Scheck & Bobby Martino have kept our van experience secret for all these years. I also believe the gas station attendant has kept his word. Therefore, it had to be that sneaky looking little fat guy with the dark sun glasses standing by the men's room door in the gas station at that time!!

WHAT DID I DO WITH THAT KID

SUBMITTED BY
KEVIN CORRIGAN NOTRE DAME COACH

We all know how distracted (or focused as we prefer to think of it) coaches become during the season. One day early in our season I came in the office and told my assistants at the time that I was lucky my wife didn't know what happened that morning or she would kill me. I then recounted how I had been backing into my parking spot at the office and heard a little voice pipe up from the back seat saying "What are we doing here Dad?". I had forgotten to drop off my five year old son at day care on the way to work. Thinking fast I told him "We're sneaking up on them today Will", and we then walked to his day care which thankfully was located on the Notre Dame campus.

One of my assistants at that time was Steve Ciccarone, the son of the infamous Henry Ciccarone, coach of the Johns Hopkins University lacrosse team. He laughed and told me that his dad used to take him and his brothers to school every day when he was a kid, and they were used to him being distracted. One day they were on their way to school with the three boys buckled in the backseat and they approached a stop light where a car was sitting ahead of them. Steve said his dad appeared to not see the car and never slowed down as they slammed into the back of the car. After the dust settled one of the Chic's younger sons spoke up, yelling "Shot, Score, Yea blue jay!!" cracking them all up.

JERRY THELEN

SUBMITTED BY
CARL RUNK

Jerry Thelen was a lifetime friend and one of the funniest people I have ever known. He never lacked the ability to come up with a story or joke that could knock you to your knees along with being related to the subject you were discussing. Jerry was an all-american lacrosse player at the University of Maryland in the late 50's – early 60's. He was also a very successful high school lacrosse coach for over 30 years in Baltimore County, Md. A great coach, a good friend, and I miss him very much.

I remember when we were to graduate from St. Michael's grammar school in 1950. Brother Joe Weber called both Jerry and I into his office. He asked us what our future intentions were. "What are you going to do now that your leaving St. Michaels?" We mentioned we were going to attend "Mt. St Josephs' prep school". St. Joe's was a prestigious catholic high school in Baltimore. Brother Joe was a very serious and highly religious man and it was out of character to hear him burst into laughter at that time the way he did. With tears in his eyes he responded, "You guys have got to be kidding!!! You'll never be able to get in

St. Joe's, ….. not with those grades!!" He told us our best bet was to attend the district public high school, Patterson Park High School, that they had to take us in, and that after we flunked out the first semester we would end up at the local steel mill , Bethlehem Steel in Sparrows Point. So much for grammar school counseling!! And would you believe he needed a masters degree to tell us that?!!

After telling our friends of our change of mind and our decision to go to Patterson, … like it was our choice!! … we were informed that before entrance to the Patterson school we would be tested and the results of the testing would determine what curriculum we would follow.

There were 3 curriculums at the school. The academic courses- designed for the smartest kids and located on the 3rd floor, the commercial courses which were located on the 2nd floor – designed for the business oriented, and the technical course - which was not even located on the first floor but down in that dark dungy basement! This was the area where promising students could be found engaging their intelligence with subjects related to car engines, wood carpentry, metal shop, printing, and chewing "Red Man" tobacco while doing that … just to name a few. Not that there is anything wrong with that. We both agreed that the technical course was not the way to go for success oriented individuals such as the two of us!! But were we personally capable of acquiring a test score which would assure us entry into the academic curriculum? We didn't think so. It was at that time we decided to formulate a plan of attack and to stick to it the best we could. Our plan made sense …. especially at that time. We would go to the test center early and search out an individual who had the characteristics of an intelligent student. A person who wore glasses would be perfect. Why? Because, in our rationalizing, any person wearing glasses at that young an age must have spent a lot of time reading and, therefore, had to be highly intelligent. And would you believe we struck it rich!! Right in the front row was a skinny nerdish looking student wearing glasses. This was going to be our tow-line to success. Jerry took a seat position on the nerd's left while I did the same on his right. Our field position was perfect and we were in the zone! Later, we came out of the testing center slapping fives!! We were going to be in the academic curriculum on the third floor!

Approximately a week and a half later, Jerry visited me at my home and asked if I got my acceptance letter from our new school. I told him I did and I asked him what was his score on the test we had just taken. He proudly told me he received an 81 which was, to us, a low B or a B-. I was quick to tell him I received an 82. "We socked it to them, Jerry … We're going to be in the academic curriculum on the third floor with all those good looking co-eds!!

On the first day of school we were informed we would meet at our specific "home room" which was located at "BF – Room 12". When we asked where "BF" was the response we received would tear our hearts out. "BF" meant <u>basement floor!</u> When we arrived at the class room, I remember telling the instructor "there must be some kind of mistake … we scored an 82 on the test, which was an adequate score and, therefore, we should be assigned on the 3rd floor in the academic program." The instructor, a stone masochist, seemed to lack compassion and derived pleasure in informing us that the test taken was not based on the 60 to 100 point grading system but "it was your I.Q. assessment and, therefore, your placement here is the correct move!! Mr. Runk, Mr. Thelen … Please take your seats!!" For a short period of time, I broke out in a cold sweat and had flashbacks of Brother Joe's laughing and telling us where we would end up. As Jerry and I took our seats, starting out on our four to six year high school journey, (in the basement!) you'll never guess who we sat next to!! You've got it!!! …… that skinny little four-eyed nerd!! That dumb ass little dip who let us down!! We sure messed up on that plan of success. We did eventually get on the third floor. There were numerous times, going to the cafeteria on the elevator, we would stop on the third floor and use the men's restroom to wash the car grease from our hands and face.

For your information, the skinny little four-eyed dip got a job at "Fisher Bodies Chevrolet" as a carburetor mechanic.

RUNK'S MOUNTAIN

SUBMITTED BY
KEN SMOOT TOWSON LACROSSE '70

On our southern trip to North Carolina when we played North Carolina and Duke, we stayed in a motel half way between Durham and Raleigh. We beat North Carolina, our rival that year, and had a day off before playing Duke. The team gathered in our captain Jimmy Saxon room and started to celebrate. About eleven that night two other players, Jon Sothoron, Ted Tremper and I decided to hitch hike to Durham, Raleigh. I don't think we knew how hard that was going to be! After standing by the highway for about 15 minutes acting stupid, I noticed a highway patrol trooper sitting across the highway. When I saw him he flipped on the lights and came flying across the median. We ran like hell, Ted got caught, and I fell in a deep hole and hurt myself. It's the fastest I've ever seen Sothoron run!! The trooper woke Coach Runk up to confirm Ted was with us to play against Duke the next day.

I couldn't play against Duke because of my leg. Coach Runk assumed I was injured in the North Carolina game.

So everything was OK until we returned to school and a few days later Coach Runk saw the school newspaper, The Towerlight, with a headline that read, "Smoot hurt while eluding police". It was "Runk's Mountain" for me after that. "Runk's Mountain" was the name of the highest hill in Towson and a fantastic conditioning tool for Coach Runk when practice wasn't going correct!! We did, however, beat Duke while on the trip, so all's well that ends well. I vaguely remember we did some damage to the motel that night. It was a special time, great fun, and a good story for cocktail parties.

NEVER TRUST YOUR JUDGEMENT

SUBMITTED BY
CARL RUNK

A few years ago I received a phone call from a salesperson requesting some support. It seems he and a friend had started an athletic clothing company in a basement apartment while they were attending the University of Maryland. He wanted to know if we would try to sell their t-shirts at our lacrosse camp. In return, he would supply each member of our staff with a complimentary embroidered shirt. It was his intention to gain exposure and since our camp drew young athletes from across the nation, numbering over 600 participants, this seemed to be a worthwhile venture. He also mentioned we might want to consider buying stock in the company. I agreed to help and do everything possible to support their cause. One thing for sure, I wasn't thinking about buying any stock! Our staff wore the t-shirts during the course of the week and we really tried to push the shirts at the camp store but to no avail. For some reason these shirts did not appeal to the kids. At the end of camp all the shirts were boxed and returned to the company. I contacted the salesman and expressed my thanks for the complimentary shirts. I also mentioned how sorry I was that we couldn't sell many of the shirts. The shirts just didn't catch on. Maybe next year.

The following year I tried to contact the salesman about the possibility of selling their product at camp again. The attempt was unsuccessful. I can honestly say that I was looking for the free staff t-shirts. Sure saved us a lot of money! I received an e-mail later in the summer from the salesman stating since the company was so busy they were unable to help us. He also said to <u>"Watch for our commercial during the Super Bowl game.</u> We believe it's going to give us a tremendous boost in sales." Would you believe that little company, which started in an apartment in College Park, Md., And with a name like <u>"Under Armour"</u>… has become one of the largest sports apparell companies in the nation!!!

Being a coach for over 47 years and I violate one the most important principles in coaching: <u>"Never underestimate your opponent!"</u>

At a recent party and social gathering I mentioned this story to a very good friend and ex-player of mine, Bob Griebe. Bob, vice president of the largest lacrosse equipment company in the nation, said "You know, the same thing happened to us. They came to us wanting to know if we'd be interested in their company and we told them we weren't. Who the hell would want to buy a tight fitting polyester t-shirt?!! They'll never make it!" Famous last words!! Evidently, a whole lot of people were interested!!! Should have bought the damn stock!! (Wouldn't have had to write this book!!!)

THE NEW SPORTS JACKET

SUBMITTED BY
CARL RUNK

In building a program, quite often it is important to achieve success through constant promotion of every and any phase of the program at your disposal. This would, without a doubt, include speaking engagements.

Years ago, after practice I was on my way home in the evening. I had called my wife, Joan, telling her I was to speak at an athletic banquet and I was on a strict schedule, that if she could have everything ready, including my dinner and clothes, it would really help my time-line. On arrival, Joan had everything prepared. She is so efficient in these matters! She even informed me that she had bought a new sports coat for me. I was ready to "knock em out!!" Everything went well at the banquet. I was on time, mixed well with the parents, and enjoyed talking about our program to the players. The M.C. introduced me as the guest speaker and I was ready to make my mark! I have a tendency to use my hands quite a bit when I speak and it wasn't far into my talk I found myself with both hands above my shoulders. This isn't unusual, with the exception that I noticed something dangling from my right coat sleeve. It seems my wonderful wife overlooked taking the tags off the jacket sleeve and there it stood, for the whole world to see, hanging down in a very obvious manner! I hesitated for a few seconds trying to regroup, just staring at the price tag. Everyone was aware of what was taking place. Finally, I said the first thing that came to my mind. "Oh, that reminds me …. I have to get this jacket back to the store by nine o'clock!! I only rented it for 3 hours!!!" The crowd let out with a loud comforting laugh. They actually thought it was a part of my routine. It was the last time I trusted Joan with my clothes. Damn shame I have to do everything myself!!

APPLYING THE PAVLOV THEORY

SUBMITTED BY
CARL RUNK

How often have we committed an action that served a purpose yet left us with a guilty feeling. I've been there, done that, many times. One of the times occurred while I was in my final semester of my senior year at the University of Arizona. It was also my first year as the school's lacrosse coach. (Probably because no one knew anything about lacrosse in Arizona!) At the time, my wife Joan and I lived in a half of a quonset hut in an area called "Polo Village" right off of campus. This area was highly convenient and available for military personnel only. Our neighbors lived about 30 feet away from us. The wife, a highly attractive young woman, was a stunt woman for any movies that were being filmed in Tucson. The husband, besides being a full time student, played the drums in a local band. Thank goodness he didn't have to practice at home!! I don't think I could've taken both the twins crying and him banging the drums at the same time! They were good people and we talked occasionally.

Our twins were at the age were they crawled all over the place so in order to give them some playing experience I built them a sandbox about four feet by four feet. It was great fun for them and they looked forward to getting in the box every day. It was just a short time later when I came home after lacrosse practice my wife, Joan, informed me that we had a problem. It seems our neighbors cat, "Foxy", was becoming very familiar with our boys' sand box. Therefore, according to Joan, it was my duty to break the news to our neighbors and see if we could find a solution. I confronted my neighbor, Joe, and explained the problem. "Joe, your cat is doing a number in our boys' sand box! Is there any way you can keep the cat in the house so we can eliminate the problem!? Or do you have any possible solutions?" His answer was very unsympathetic, to say the least. "Carl, I don't know what to tell you. Cats are known for relieving themselves in sand boxes if they are available." I then asked him if he could build a box outside or a small one for the house. His response was, "No, I aint got time for that!!" He then turned and walked back to his hut. I was stunned by his reaction and thought to myself, "If he thinks that box is big enough for my kids and his cat ... he's got another thought coming. There was no way this was going to continue!! Who the hell does he think he is!!!? I devised a plan that I felt would eliminate the problem. Our bathroom window was just above the play box. I went to the hardware store and bought chicken wire which could be laid completely around the box. I also had an electric shaven razor that was broke. (At this point, I think you're starting to figure this out!!) I removed the wire from the razor and attached the razor end of the wire to the chicken wire. The other side was plugged inside the bathroom outlet. It was now time to patiently wait for "foxy" to make his appearance. And here he came, strutting like he owned the neighborhood. As the cat came into the sun-light he paused to stretch. There he stood with his front paws stretched to the front, his chest, lightly touching the grass, and his hips in very high position. It must have been time to relieve himself as he strutted toward the box. I peeked out the window and waited for the proper moment. There it was!! "Foxy" had all four paws inside the "war" zone. As I hit a quick on/off of the switch, that cat let out one hell of a yell and as I can recall when he jumped, he was eye-level with me. There he was in mid-air. His fur stood out stiff like a porky-pine, and his eyes looked like two green grapes in a glass of butter milk!! I truly believe I had pulled the chicken wire inside the window before that cat hit the ground! His journey back to his hut was the quickest thing I've ever seen!! It was not the best way to solve a problem but I was a young man and very protective of my kids, and it was the only thing I could think of! If it would work for Pavlov it would work for me. After that unfortunate experience, "Foxy" would come out in the morning and afternoon, strutting his stuff, but for some unknown reason, never returned to the sand box, always going in a different direction, away from our house.

ANDY NELSON

SUBMITTED BY
CARL RUNK

I can truthfully say Andy Nelson is one of the most humble and down to earth people I have ever known. He is a soft spoken individual with an impressively slow southern accent. When talking to Andy, at times, you already know what he is going to say before he finishes the sentence. However, you very politely wait for him to finish. Andy was a member of the "World Champion Baltimore Colts" football team as a defensive corner-back. He was also selected to the All-Pro team. Andy, like so many others who participated at that time, is considered a pioneer of National Football League. Members of teams back then laid the foundation for the tremendous growth and spectator interest that is witnessed in the game today. Players, at that time, participated for the love of the game, when salaries weren't that much and, at the close of the season, they were compelled to find part time employment somewhere in the city in order to survive. Andy, after struggling for many years, was able to create a restaurant business that has become very popular in the Baltimore area. Anyone craving barbecue ribs and outstanding barbecued pulled pork and beef sandwiches will head over to Andy's without hesitation. I recall talking with Andy about the State of Maryland Barbecue Competition held each year in Bel Air, Md. Does he enter that competition? "Every year!" was his response. "Carl, we load up all the vans with everything needed and head on over to start the fires and grills a day ahead of time. In the evening several of the judges for the contest come over to our tent to talk for a while and I feed them dinner. When they're finished, the first thing they tell me is, *"Andy, that was some of the best damn barbecue I've ever tasted!! That was simply fantastic!!"* I feel good about their enjoying my cooking and I look forward to the competition the next day. And Carl, would you believe, … when we start the competition …. at the end of the day when it's all over … I never win or even place in that damn contest!! This has been going on for years and every year it's the same old thing!!! I don't think I'm going to feed 'em anymore!"

We talked for some time about the number of concussions that occur in today's game. Andy shared with me some of his football situations. One story that I found quite humorous was when the Colts were playing the Green Bay Packers. The game, throughout, was filled with hard hitting action and at one particular time Green Bay's running back, Jim Taylor, who was known for the punishment he could, and would, inflict on the oncoming tackler, came through the line with only Andy available to stop him. Andy thought, "If I hit him high he'll run over me or carry me to the goal line. I'll need to tackle him low in order to stop him. Unfortunately, Andy, when attempting to tackle Jim Taylor low, met with one of Jims' knees to the side of the helmet with such a force it left Andy semi-unconscious and dizzy as hell. As he got up from the ground he returned to the huddle. It was in the huddle Andy felt an arm come across his shoulder and he heard a voice, "Andy, are you ok? Andy replied "Sure … Why?" "Because you're in the wrong huddle, Andy ... You belong over there on the other side of the scrimmage line!"

Andy finished up by stating, "And you know, Carl, I never came out of the game. It was just the way the game was played back then."

Brenda's hole in one

BRENDA

SUBMITTED BY
CARL RUNK

The old expression, "The fruit doesn't fall far from the tree", is extremely accurate when describing our daughter, Brenda. My wife Joan and I have always felt we were blessed with a gift from the Lord when Brenda entered our lives.

Brenda was a teenager when we both were traveling through Baltimore en-route to her girlfriends' house where she would stay for the week-end. As a typical protective parent, this would be an ideal opportunity for me to re-enforce important moral values in a non-asserting manner. I should stay away from the preaching mode and have her believe this is no more than a warm "father/daughter discussion. And what better way to accomplish this task than to involve someone else's daughter and the negative decisions that poor creature made. That was it! I was ready to make a life-long impression on my Brenda! My next move was to introduce this tear-jerking story. "Hey Bren, did I tell you about my friends daughter?" It was at this time I started to concoct a story of a young lady who was at the crossroads of decision regarding right and wrong. This young lady chose the path that was not conducive to the righteous way. I continued to tell Brenda how the young lady was unable to distinguish between "doing something because it feels good, or doing something because it was the right thing to do," while citing examples of each!! Enjoying a short feeling of accomplishment, I tried to involve Brenda in the discussion by asking her opinion. She quickly leaned over to my side of the car, pointed out the window and asked, "Hey dad, what's the name of that building over there"? Highly irritated, I responded, "Brenda ... didn't you hear anything I was talking about"? It was at this time she sat back in her seat and burst out laughing. "Dad, it's a good thing you are in coaching 'cause you would never have made a good psycho- analyst!!"

Isn't it strange how I started out trying to play with her mind and end up with her playing with mine. Maybe she was right.

THE HOLE IN ONE

SUBMITTED BY
CARL RUNK

It was at Myrtle Beach, during our summer vacation, when we decided that Joan, me, and Brenda would go to the Par 3 golf course and have a great afternoon. After picking up the necessary equipment, (clubs, balls, &tees), we were off to the greens. I, though not being highly knowledgeable about the game of golf, had the basic understanding about addressing the ball and how to hold the club. This information, therefore and unselfishly, would be shared with my wife and daughter. This was a first for Brenda as she had never been to a golf course before and had limited experience at the local putt-putt! It was up to me to try to explain the game to her and why it was more beneficial to hold the club a specific way than holding it like a field hockey club, with the hands far apart. It was at the 6th hole that I finally said, "If the hand position on the club seems to be hindering you, just remember to aim the club head at the target, grab the club like a baseball bat, and swing like hell!!" As Brenda addressed the ball at the tee, <u>in her shower clogs</u>, she did exactly what I said. She grabbed the club like a baseball bat and swung like hell at the ball. I will never forget the trajectory of that ball. It seemed to travel the first hundred yards like it was on a frozen rope! It then hit the turf with aggression, rolled to the green and found its resting place in the cup!! My daughter, who has never been on a golf course in her life, hit a 136 yard <u>hole in one</u>!! We were simply elated and excited. I think Brenda wet her pants, she was so excited. As we came back into the club house we told the attendant and all in attendance that Brenda hit a hole in one. An elderly gentleman seated on a bench exclaimed, "Young lady … You have never played before and you just hit a hole in one? … Do you realize what you have done?? … I've been playing for 46 years and haven't hit one yet!!"

I attribute her success to good coaching!

FATHER JIM

SUBMITTED BY
CARL RUNK

After a hard fought Saturday evening contest I was in my office preparing for the coming week's game. I decided that before I go to the office on Sunday afternoon in preparation for the week, I would do something around the house, Sunday morning, in order to keep everyone happy.

At the time, I was living in Hamilton, a part of the city made up of old individual homes. My neighbors were just great and I considered myself to be very fortunate. On Sunday morning I decided that I would attempt to fix the motorized lawn mower that seemed to be giving me a problem. I was not sure what the problem was but I was determined find the answer. As I am not too qualified at taking things apart or putting them back together, my system was to place a piece of canvas, 4' X 4', alongside the lawn mower. As I removed each intricate part, it was strategically placed on the canvas in a right to left, front row to back row manner. This way, I would know exactly where to begin when I attempted to put the gadget back together.

I have found that older people have one thing in common. When someone else is at work, they seemed to be drawn to the work area to watch, give advice, or jump right in there! Father Jim was no exception. Father Jim was a retired catholic priest who lived with his sister, occasionally, right next door to me. A very pleasant man who could be heard, at times, yelling and arguing with that woman who seemed to always have the right answer. It always ended in a friendly way with Father Jim blessing her before he left for church. Both were very dear to each other.

As I was in the beginning stages of my mechanical endeavor, Father Jim came over to see what it was that I was doing. It didn't take long before I became the "GoFer" and the Father took over. At first I thought Father Jim knew what he was doing. He seemed to lack the "intricate part, strategically placed" method I found so helpful but maybe that was his way of doing things. He would just unscrew something and throw it on the canvas! I began to wonder if the old timer knew what the hell he was doing. After a short frustrating period of time, Father, sweating profusely, backed up, scratching his head, looked at me and stated "Carl, I truthfully don't know what the problem is!! You'll have to forgive me Son, I have to leave and go serve the twelve o'clock mass at church." With that being said, he quickly turned and walked away, leaving me standing there in a bewildered state of mind. As I looked down at the many dis-assembled pieces which were scattered all over my strategically placed mat, I thought "Would this have happened to me if I were a Baptist?!!" Since there was no way to put anything back together, I simply took the four corners of the mat ... tied them together ... and dumped both the mat and the frame remains of the mower in the back of the truck, to be dumped as soon as possible. I then did something I should have done a long time before. I purchased a new lawn mower down at Sears! When I think about this ordeal and Father Jim, I often think to myself it could have been worse. Thank the Lord I wasn't working on my truck!!

Old proverb ... "Good fences make good neighbors!!"

Made in the USA
Middletown, DE
24 September 2015